The Fundamentals of
Literacy Coaching

The Fundamentals of
Literacy Coaching

Amy Sandvold
Maelou Baxter

Association for Supervision and Curriculum Development
Alexandria, Virginia USA

Association for Supervision and Curriculum Development
1703 N. Beauregard St. • Alexandria, VA 22311-1714 USA
Phone: 800-933-2723 or 703-578-9600 • Fax: 703-575-5400
Web site: www.ascd.org • E-mail: member@ascd.org
Author guidelines: www.ascd.org/write

Gene R. Carter, *Executive Director;* Nancy Modrak, *Director of Publishing;* Julie Houtz, *Director of Book Editing & Production;* Ernesto Yermoli, *Project Manager;* Cathy Guyer, *Senior Graphic Designer;* Valerie Younkin, *Desktop Publishing Specialist;* Sarah Plumb, *Production Specialist*

Printed in the United States of America. Cover art copyright © 2008 by ASCD. ASCD publications present a variety of viewpoints. The views expressed or implied in this book should not be interpreted as official positions of the Association.

All Web links in this book are correct as of the publication date below but may have become inactive or otherwise modified since that time. If you notice a deactivated or changed link, please e-mail books@ascd.org with the words "Link Update" in the subject line. In your message, please specify the Web link, the book title, and the page number on which the link appears.

PAPERBACK ISBN: 978-1-4166-0677-2   ASCD product #107084   s4/08

Also available as an e-book through ebrary, netLibrary, and many online booksellers (see Books in Print for the ISBNs).

Quantity discounts for the paperback edition only: 10–49 copies, 10%; 50+ copies, 15%; for 1,000 or more copies, call 800-933-2723, ext. 5634, or 703-575-5634. For desk copies: member@ascd.org.

Library of Congress Cataloging-in-Publication Data
Sandvold, Amy, 1971–
  The fundamentals of literacy coaching / Amy Sandvold and Maelou Baxter.
    p. cm.
  Includes bibliographical references and index.
  ISBN 978-1-4166-0677-2 (pbk. : alk. paper) 1. Reading teachers—In-service training—United States. 2. Teachers—Professional relationships—United States. I. Baxter, Maelou, 1940– II. Title.
  LB2844.1.R4S26 2008
  428.4071'5—dc22

                                                                                2007050939

18 17 16 15 14 13 12 11 10 09 08   1 2 3 4 5 6 7 8 9 10 11 12

This book is dedicated to the students,

the ultimate beneficiaries of literacy coaching.

Why else would we be doing this?

The Fundamentals of Literacy Coaching

Acknowledgments

We would like to acknowledge some brilliant people who have inspired and coached us together in our common coaching experiences and influenced us individually. This book evolved and exists today as a result of their collective contribution and common dedication to helping all students achieve a life rich in literacy. It would be impossible to highlight all of these people and institutions, but we must attempt the impossible.

First, we acknowledge the efforts of Carol Watson, our partner in everything and part of Reading Excellence. Were it not for her new life as a very busy Reading Recovery teacher leader, she would have written this book with us. Her work and inspiration, both personal and professional, are woven through the pages.

Our expert friends:

To David Moore, who taught Maelou how to develop and hang onto a thought.

To Penny Beed of the University of Northern Iowa, who believed in Amy and encouraged her to have a voice in the world of literacy. Penny worked alongside both of us to develop and refine our coaching efforts.

To Christine Canning, also of the University of Northern Iowa, who first told Amy that she had important things to say and expected to hear about it in the future. Thank you for the inspiration and challenge.

To Marcia Scheppele, Salli Forbes, Mary Ann Poparad, Sylvia Boehmke, Renee DeBerg, Jan Rowray, Karla Ostby, Mary Hoffman, and Bonnie Hoewing, who offered their literacy expertise in working with both children and adults.

To Judy Jeffrey and Ted Stillwell, for supporting and dedicating themselves to local control in the state of Iowa.

To Nina Carran, for inspiring districts to work toward workplace professional development.

To Paul Cahill, Teresa McCune, Sandra Johnson, Donna Eggleston, and Geri McMahon, for providing Amy with positive leadership and a political foundation.

To P. David Pearson and Barbara Taylor, who, as part of CIERA, inspired our efforts. We still believe that literacy coaching is an essential part of helping teachers and students to "Beat the Odds."

Our own professional coaches:

We were fortunate enough to select two outstanding people to coach us and provide professional development to our teachers. Gail Saunders-Smith and Angela Maiers were more than trainers; they revolutionized the thinking and practice of the teachers in the districts in which we worked, and provided both us and the teachers with expert coaching.

Forward-thinking administrators:

To John Van Pelt, who supported us in every way possible.

To Loleta Montgomery, Helen Melichar, Bob Wright, Ron Morlan, Bernard Cooper, and Peg Frey, the principals of the Reading Excellence schools, who supported us and helped us to develop our coaching effort.

To Arlis Swarzendruber, who, as superintendent, did what all wise leaders do—he recognized a good thing, and he let it happen.

Our "bosses":

To Rachael Goodwin, Dorothy Winter, and Patrick Clancy, who supported Maelou, taught her, and let her do her job—mostly as she saw it.

To Tony Reid, one of Amy's "bosses," who saw the possibilities of workplace coaching and took a risk in implementing a new and different way of supporting and increasing teacher expertise at his school.

Dedicated educators who connected us to the realities of the classroom:

To the Key Teachers, who helped us write a district guidebook and served as advisors.

To the classroom teachers, both reluctant and willing, who allowed themselves to be coached, and who taught us as much as we taught them. Amy would specifically like to acknowledge the positive energy and early contributions to this book from her former colleagues Sue Oldani, Mary Egli, Laurie Wyckoff, Linda Hansen, Jill Schulte, Joan Trebon, Joanne White, and Jackie Rubendall.

To Maelou's Literacy Breakfast friends, Maureen Oates, Peggy Pruisner, and Robin Kautz, who educated, supported, and inspired her. It was well worth going to breakfast at 6:00 a.m. every Wednesday morning.

Other important literacy advocates:

To the secretaries, paraprofessionals, custodians, and other "supporters" who helped us in more ways than we can count. Our special friend, cameraman Dan Evanson, actually became part of our initiative, and by the end was even answering the questions!

Our editors:

To Carolyn Pool, who liked our book and talked us through its coming of age with humor and great expertise.

To Ernesto Yermoli, for expert listening, talking with Amy's students, and approaching this task with a collaborative mindset.

Maelou's special acknowledgments:

To my mother, who was the first to show me that it's all about education. She was right then, and she's right now.

To my family, for always supporting me, being proud of me, and letting me do "my thing," no matter how crazy it may have seemed to them. To Jen, Kare, Jeff, and Steve; to the "grands," Jessica, Lincoln, Abbie, Zach, and Zoë; and most of all to Ken, who doesn't always understand why I want to do what I want to do, but who always loves me and supports me in the doing.

Amy's special acknowledgments:

First and foremost, to my husband, Jeff, who tells it like it is and challenges me to be the best I can be. You are truly my ultimate coach and best friend. Thank you for supporting me through the writing of this book and the other professional "itches" that I get, and for being the excellent husband and dedicated father that you are to our four children, Houston, Andrew, Anna and Lauren. Thank you, baby Lauren! Bed rest after you were born gave me the time to put my passion to the page and write, write, write!

To Kasey Eller. Thank you, Kasey, for getting up early every day to run several miles and solve what's wrong with education, for giving me insight into excellent teaching through what you share, and, most important, for being a great friend.

To Angela Maiers—thank you for your true friendship and for your smart mind! You understand how I think. I greatly cherish our friendship and exchanges of dialogue around literacy and learning.

To my in-laws, Jessica and Matt Switzer, Jennifer and Brad Nelson, and Keith and Louise Sandvold. Thank you for your support through the writing of this book and the time you spent helping with the kids.

Finally, to my parents, Marjorie and Kenneth Keller. You taught me early on that if you believe it, you will achieve it. Most of all, you modeled and continue to demonstrate integrity. If I can someday live a life with half the integrity you demonstrate, then I know I have truly succeeded.

Foreword

When I first read the draft of *The Fundamentals of Literacy Coaching*, a wave of memories and emotions overwhelmed me. Six years ago, I was one of four elementary school principals who initiated the Reading Excellence program in Iowa's Waterloo Community Schools. I had a lot to learn about such concepts as walk-throughs, gradual release of responsibility, scaffolding, peer coaching, modeling, and cognitive coaching—all while leading the staff of what was then the district's largest elementary school.

In 1998, an intensive curriculum audit concluded that our district needed to develop a systematic, research-based approach to reading instruction that included ongoing teacher support and professional development based on best practices. The district committed to this goal by assembling a development team that spent countless days developing a consistent K–12 reading and language arts curriculum for the district.

Now that we had a curriculum, we needed a system to ensure that teachers would gain a deep understanding of it and routinely apply its suggested strategies. With funding from a major grant, we targeted four schools in which to implement the Reading Excellence program. The schools chosen shared the following characteristics:

- A combined student mobility rate of 60 to 70 percent
- A student population that was 70 to 80 percent low-income
- A 4th grade reading proficiency level of less than 48 percent
- Different reading instructional approaches and materials from building to building
- A tendency to offer disjointed professional development with little or no follow-up

The reading coaches at these schools served as instructional specialists, resource providers, data coaches, and adult learning facilitators, working alongside teachers to model, observe, and provide feedback.

Over the next three years, the four schools made consistent gains in reading achievement, leading the district to implement reading coaches in all K–8 schools. By 2004, the district was being honored by Iowa's First in the Nation in Education Foundation for our efforts to improve student reading skills. In accepting this award for the district, I spoke the following words:

> I accept this award on behalf of each child in our district, irrespective of socioeconomic status, ethnicity, or learning

challenge, who can now pick up a book, read the words
. . . create meaning around and among the words . . . and
be able to say, "I am a reader."

Through this book, Amy Sandvold and Maelou Baxter continue
their invaluable work on a grander scale. *The Fundamentals of Literacy Coaching* should be required reading in any district that is
considering implementing or improving a reading coach model.

—Loleta A. Montgomery
Elementary Curriculum Coordinator
Waterloo Community Schools
Waterloo, Iowa

Introduction

························

Dreams are how we figure out where we want to go.

Life is how we get there.

—Kermit the Frog

Looking back, it seems that I started down the road to literacy coaching long ago.

I had planned to be a high school English teacher, and I did my student teaching in middle school. Soon, I began also teaching adult basic education and GED classes. The longer I taught adults, the more I realized that many of them couldn't read well enough to meet the demands of their daily lives. I enrolled in university to help me figure out "this reading thing." Though I ended up with a doctorate, I never *did* figure it out!

After graduating, I became a Title I reading teacher, then a consultant supporting other Title I reading teachers. With the advent of schoolwide projects, I soon began to work with classroom teachers as well. Much of what I have contributed to this book I learned from working with these teachers. I saw what little effect "sit-and-get" in-service training had on instruction. As a perennial student, I learned more and more about workshop versus workplace professional development, and I realized that only the combination of both has any real chance of making a difference for teachers and students.

When I was asked to head up the federal Reading Excellence initiative for Iowa's Waterloo Community Schools, I realized immediately that we would need reading coaches. Luckily I found two brilliant people to work with in that capacity. Amy, of course, was one of them. The other was Carol Watson, who was being trained as a Reading Recovery teacher leader but would otherwise have written this book with us. I continued to learn through them as well as through the teachers with whom we worked.

—*Maelou Baxter*

* * *

Having worked as an elementary classroom teacher, a K–8 Title I reading teacher, and a combination reading teacher/literacy coach, I know what it is like both to be coached and to coach others. I also served as a supervisor of graduate and undergraduate students working with children with reading difficulties at the University of Northern Iowa, where I coached teachers in reflective, diagnostic instruction. Later, at the Iowa Department of Education, my philosophy of "coaching the teacher as reflective practitioner" was strengthened by coaching gurus Robert Garmston and Bruce Wellman, who taught me their model of cognitive coaching. I went on to apply lessons from this training to the over 100 school districts that I've served as a consultant for the Bureau of School Improvement. As a liaison for the state reading initiative, I affirmed my commitment to in-the-workplace modeling, coaching, and follow-up.

My passion for literacy coaching increased tenfold after working in the trenches in the Waterloo Community Schools, where I served as a full-time literacy coach and helped create a peer-coaching framework.

—*Amy Sandvold*

* * *

Through our sometimes painful experiences, we have collected valuable knowledge that can help guide the efforts of literacy coaches and the administrators who oversee their work. These experiences, the excitement and satisfaction we have found in them, and our desire to spare you at least *some* of the pain that we have endured have encouraged us to share with you the fundamentals of literacy coaching.

—*Maelou and Amy*

Be Prepared

If I had eight hours to chop down a tree, I'd spend six sharpening my axe.

—Abraham Lincoln

Although committing to literacy coaching takes a lot of money and mind power, it's well worthwhile, because coaching has been shown to increase teacher expertise (Van Pelt & Poparad, 2006), and teacher expertise in reading instruction improves student reading achievement (Allington, 2002). The process does not have to be complicated, but it does require some forethought.

Know Your Purpose

It's *all* about student achievement. Student achievement results from expert teaching, and it is the purpose of coaching to *promote* expert teaching. It's a simple formula—

Literacy Coaching → Expert Teaching → Student Achievement

—but it's easy, as you become more and more involved in the details, to forget the ultimate purpose. It's not to make teachers happy, it's not to fulfill the requirements of the state department of education, it's not to satisfy your own administrators—it's to increase student achievement. For a literacy coaching effort to produce the expert teaching that can accomplish this, a good, basic plan should be in place from the start.

Here are some questions to consider prior to setting up a coaching initiative:

- Are there special barriers to expert teaching in your school or district for which you must plan? For example, are there inconsistent instructional practices or curriculum changes that require additional teacher training? Is there high student or teacher mobility?
- What will the coaching model look like?

• Will coaches be hired at several district schools or only at one?
• Will the literacy coaches also work as part-time reading teachers?

Maelou was working as a Title I reading consultant in Iowa's Waterloo Community Schools when she was asked to help write a grant application for a reading improvement initiative. She agreed to do what she could and ended up helping create a whole new reading framework for the district, including a reading and language arts curriculum complete with objectives, materials, and sample lessons.

When Maelou first began working on the initiative, over 100 different instructional methods were being used in the district's 14 elementary schools. It was possible to go from one 2nd grade classroom to another at the same school and see different methods and books employed. Lacking sufficient guidance, the teachers had figured out for themselves what methods and materials would work best for their students.

Obviously, the district needed a consistent instructional approach and quality professional development for the teachers. Research and experience suggested that the teachers would need ongoing, on-site support to put into practice a literacy coaching framework. The district only had the money to hire coaches for the four schools that had received the grant, so the coaching model had to be devised on a small scale and only later developed into a districtwide effort. The budget restriction ended up being a blessing in disguise, as it provided an opportunity to work out the model's kinks and to compare the four targeted schools to the rest.

Maelou realized early on that coaching had to be a part of the plan. For too long she had seen teachers struggle alone, wanting to do their best for their students but not always knowing what the best was. These teachers needed a critical, supportive friend to stand beside them and help them be their best.

Choose the Right Coach

Before starting a search for a coach or even writing a job description, administrators should familiarize themselves with the professional standards for coaches. The International Reading Association states that, at a minimum, coaches must meet the association's standards for reading specialists and obtain their reading specialist certification within three years (International Reading Association, 2004). In the meantime, reading specialists should directly supervise coaches who do not have the certification.

Coaches need to exhibit flexibility, an ability to work with others, good listening skills, and other personal attributes that can't be discerned from a transcript or diploma. These attributes are just as important as academic knowledge and should be assessed through interviews and discussions with the prospective coaches' references. To ensure that only qualified coaches are considered, the district should draft a job description that explains the role in detail, such as in Figure 1.1.

Making certain everyone is familiar with the job description will help avoid uncomfortable situations. For example, a coach should never be directed to observe a teacher and provide the principal with feedback: even if the coach does not serve as an evaluator—and we highly recommend that he or she not do so—providing feedback to the principal can damage the trust between teacher

FIGURE 1.1	Sample Reading Coach Job Description

Teacher Support

• Builds good interpersonal relations and establishes positive rapport with colleagues

• Proactively supports teachers

• Helps teachers implement the reading and language arts curriculum guide activities

• Selects and gathers resources and related materials to enhance and support the reading and language arts curriculum guides

• Uses cognitive coaching and other district-recommended strategies for small-group instruction and working with words

• Helps teachers plan lessons, observes teaching in action, provides feedback, and models best practices for small-group reading instruction and working with words

• Observes and assesses students in class and helps teachers problem solve as needed

Program Facilitation

• Provides coaching in the development, implementation, and monitoring of research-based practices in reading and language arts

• Attends some team leader meetings

• Communicates and publishes deadlines for forms (e.g., implementation logs, time sheets)

• Helps determine professional development needs in the area of language arts and provides professional development as appropriate

• Organizes professional development presentations

• Participates in and supports data-driven decision making at the school and district level

(Continued)

FIGURE 1.1	Sample Reading Coach Job Description (*continued*)

Liaison with Administration

• Helps develop language arts professional development for principals

• Reports to district elementary curriculum coordinator and attends district meetings as required

• Facilitates ongoing communication with building principals

• Works cooperatively with coaches, curriculum coordinators, and assistant superintendents

• Meets with building principals regularly to plan

Data Collection/Interpretation and Assessment

• Collects, organizes, interprets, and reports data with core team

• Helps group students for instruction

• Assesses student literacy development as requested by teachers, using

    – Developmental reading assessments

    – Observation surveys

    – Qualitative reading inventories

    – Running records

and coach and set the coaching process back by several months. Coaches should do anything they can to make teachers understand that they serve as professional friends and guides, not evaluators. A productive coaching relationship requires a high degree of trust.

Finding the right coaches is crucial, and we were extremely fortunate in this respect. When Amy went to Waterloo, Iowa, as part of a state Title I audit team, Maelou asked her if she knew of anyone who would make a good reading coach. As it turned out, she was interested in coaching herself, so she joined the initiative. A second coach was still needed, however, and Maelou knew just the person: Carol Watson, who at the time was a Title I reading teacher in the district. Maelou approached Carol, who said that she was too busy working on an advanced degree and taking care of family responsibilities to consider it. Then one day, after Maelou had given up, Carol called. She said she was inspired to become a coach after watching a video of P. David Pearson discussing research from the Center for the Improvement of Early Reading Achievement (CIERA).

Get It Right at the Beginning

Any coaching plan should be flexible so that it may be adjusted for changing demands or issues that haven't been considered—after all, no matter how well you do your homework, you won't think of everything! Of course, you want to get as much right from the beginning as possible.

Develop and Nourish Ownership Among Participants

Coaches who are called upon to support a grassroots initiative are especially blessed, and they are doubly especially blessed if they have been *active participants* in the initiative, as their engagement with the process will grant them a natural sense of ownership. Unfortunately, grassroots initiatives are all too rare. It is much more likely that you will be called on to coach or support coaches within a "top-down" initiative, in which case you will need to find creative ways to help participants feel ownership.

When confronted with a top-down mandate, it is wise to create as many opportunities as possible to give teachers a sense of ownership. As Erickson (1995) has shown, school improvements follow when participants are actively involved in the decision-making process. Forming a literacy coach leadership team consisting of actual coaches can provide direction and help ensure that the group's coaching expertise is tapped. In our Reading Excellence initiative, we asked principals to identify "key teachers" to help design the project, draft a handbook for it, and discuss issues and provide support within the schools.

Clarify Responsibilities and Relationships

When administrators, teachers, and coaches work together, student achievement increases (Van Pelt & Poparad, 2006). At the school level, it is vital to consider how the literacy coach will be included in the building leadership framework. The coach's purpose is always the same: to help move building and teacher goals forward. The coach is the connection between school improvement goals and classroom implementation and as such must be involved throughout the process.

Mapping out roles and how they fit in relation to one another helps to ensure a healthy flow of communication and, by extension, greater collaboration. Such cooperation is especially critical when a new position or committee is introduced. A map of literacy-related roles and responsibilities, such as the one shown in Figure 1.2 (p. 10), can help to clarify who is in charge of what for all concerned.

When using such a map, it is especially important to address assessment. Although student evaluation should be the responsibility of teachers, literacy coaches can help the teachers to incorporate assessment into classroom routines and use the data to guide their classroom instruction. Creating a separate assessment schedule that lists exact assessment dates, types of assessments used, and the people responsible for administering them can clarify the picture for teachers.

Keep the Coaches Updated and Connected

Weekly or biweekly meetings at which literacy coaches collaborate are important for keeping the purpose of coaching in mind. A consistent framework for running the meetings is helpful. Generally speaking, there are four broad reasons for literacy coaches to hold meetings: to set goals, to analyze assessment data, to set schedules, and to support one another. If meetings are held to discuss issues beyond these, it may be a sign that coaches are being overloaded with district duties.

If there is only one coach in the district, he or she will need another kind of support group—perhaps one consisting of a few teachers and a language arts coordinator. There should always be a plan in place for ongoing support of coaches if their efforts are to be sustainable. Without such a plan, the coaching role will likely stray from the original vision.

Know Where to Look

It is a great idea to build a collection of resources for teachers and coaches. The media center can set aside some shelves for this purpose that includes both professional journals for teachers and literature for use with students. We recommend devising a simple checkout system for all books in the media center. It is also helpful to have a list of additional resources available, such as publishers, leading scholarly journals, clearinghouse Web sites, state school district Web sites, and university contacts.

FIGURE 1.2	Sample Map of District Roles and Responsibilities Related to Student Achievement		
	Leadership	Instruction	Assessment
School Principals	• Serve as instructional leaders of their schools • Provide feedback to teachers • Attend and participate in staff professional development activities • Facilitate the development and implementation of literacy-related action steps • Seek, study, and share research on instructional strategies • Schedule time and opportunities for coaching	• Evaluate teacher instruction of newly learned strategies • Practice newly learned instructional strategies • Monitor teacher implementation of newly learned strategies • Become familiar with the district glossary of common literacy language	• Allocate time during early dismissal and staff meetings for ongoing work with the literacy initiative • Study assessment results with building leadership team • Present district- and building-level assessment results to staff with building leadership team • Present district- and building-level implementation results to staff with building leadership team

FIGURE 1.2	Sample Map of District Roles and Responsibilities Related to Student Achievement (*continued*)		
	Leadership	**Instruction**	**Assessment**
Title I Coordinators and Reading Recovery Teacher Leaders	• Facilitate Title I programs • Plan and participate in professional development • Provide ongoing support to Title I teachers • Facilitate training of newly hired teachers	• May coach and observe instruction • Develop and revise the district glossary of common literacy language	• Report district reading assessment results to building principals
Literacy Coach Leadership Team	• Facilitates the literacy coaching programs • Plans and participates in professional development • Provides ongoing support for literacy coaches • Facilitates training of newly hired teachers	• Develops and revises the district glossary of common literacy language • Models newly learned strategies in classrooms • Practices newly learned strategies with other coaches • Provides teachers with references to consult when learning new strategies	• Analyzes implementation data collected by all literacy coaches with the literacy coaches • Reports district-level implementation results to literacy coaches and principals

(Continued)

FIGURE 1.2	Sample Map of District Roles and Responsibilities Related to Student Achievement (*continued*)		
	Leadership	**Instruction**	**Assessment**
Title I Reading Teachers	• Collaborate with Title I coordinators and the literacy coaches	• Provide remediation to identified struggling readers	• Administer assessments in identification of remedial students and progress of identified students • Collect building reading assessment data administered by teachers and hand in to Title I coordinators
Literacy Coaches	• Collaborate with Title I reading teachers, school principals, and the literacy coach leadership team • Actively seek opportunities to coach classroom teachers	• Model newly learned strategies in classrooms • Practice newly learned strategies with other coaches • Provide teachers with references to consult when learning new strategies	• Collect implementation data from classroom teachers and organize the data with the building leadership team • Hand in organized implementation data to the literacy coach leadership team

Sample Map of District Roles and Responsibilities Related to Student Achievement (*continued*)

FIGURE
1.2

	Leadership	Instruction	Assessment
Literacy Coaches (*continued*)	• Seek, study, and share research on instructional strategies • Facilitate literacy-related professional development at the school level		
Building Improvement Committee	• Handle the day-to-day issues of the school		• Review building-level and district-level data provided by the principal
Building Leadership Team	• Help principal facilitate school improvement planning • Seek, study, and share research on instructional strategies		• Organize implementation data collected by literacy coaches

(Continued)

FIGURE 1.2	Sample Map of District Roles and Responsibilities Related to Student Achievement (*continued*)		
	Leadership	**Instruction**	**Assessment**
Classroom Teachers	• Help coach colleagues • Implement action steps stated in school improvement literacy goals • Seek, study, and share research on instructional strategies	• Plan and deliver classroom instruction • Participate in professional development • Teach newly learned instructional strategies • Collaborate with literacy coaches and Title I teachers—plan, teach, reflect	• Collect day-to-day classroom assessment data • Administer district reading assessment(s) and hand in results to Title I teacher • Collect implementation data in own classroom and hand in to literacy coaches

Create a Common Vocabulary

"Analyze your DRA results during SAR with your CG."

What does this mean? Would somebody please call a translator! The unintelligible staff meeting agenda item above illustrates the need for everyone to speak the same language. A successful literacy coaching initiative requires teachers, coaches, administrators, and reading specialists to share a common language. What does *guided reading* mean? What's the difference between a strategy and a skill or between explicit and direct instruction? These terms should be consistently defined. Acronyms should also be clarified, perhaps in a glossary of terms made available to teachers. The literacy coach leadership team can create the glossary with input from teachers, ensuring that definitions are accurate and adding more words and translations of acronyms as needed. When we implemented the Reading Excellence initiative, key teachers, reading coaches, and Title I reading consultants compiled and published such a document and included it in a teacher guidebook (see Figure 1.3).

Maximize Resources

It is wise to avoid duplication and expense whenever possible. For example, when professional developers provide training for teachers, staff may wish to videotape the training for future reference. Though the professional developer may request a fee for being videotaped, in our experience the cost has been minimal and the tapes have been quite valuable.

Amy was videotaped both being taught coaching techniques by a professional developer and then modeling the coaches for teachers. Later she shared the tapes with teachers, as they illustrated

FIGURE 1.3	Sample Glossary Entries

homogeneous grouping: Grouping students on the basis of their shared knowledge and needs. Membership in these groups is frequently flexible.

independent reading level: The level at which a student reads orally with at least 95 percent accuracy, reads phrases with fluency and intonation, and comprehends at least 90 percent of text.

Informal Reading Inventory (IRI): The use of passages of increasing difficulty to determine students' strengths, weaknesses, and strategies in word identification and comprehension. Graded word lists are used to determine the beginning passage level.

instructional reading level: The level at which a student reads with 90 to 95 percent accuracy, reads phrases with some fluency, and comprehends at least 75 percent of text. (See also **zone of proximal development**.)

interactive writing: An individual or group practice in which students construct a sentence or other type of text in conjunction with the teacher.

internal data: School-level data on learners and the learning environment, such as standardized test results, day-to-day assessments, and current instructional practices.

that coaches are approachable and are learners as well. Literacy coaches can even develop study guides focusing on key teaching points to go with the tapes.

Assess Progress

To monitor teacher progress implementing a literacy goal or strategy, data need to be collected. Because reading teachers and literacy coaches are specifically taught to assess progress, they can help guide the collection, organization, and analysis of data. To assess teacher progress in the Reading Excellence initiative, we first drafted an implementation log and had the teachers involved fill it out. We knew we were going to have to find a way to analyze these forms, but somehow we didn't decide ahead of time who would do it and how. To make things worse, we didn't follow our own advice to keep things simple—the logs were extremely complicated and measured too many different things. Consequently, the information piled up, making it much harder to deal with when we *finally* forced ourselves to face it.

Coaches should be taught how to create implementation logs and collect and organize data themselves. A "data day" can be held to train coaches in this regard. At one of the districts in which Amy worked as a coach, all coaches were given their own laptops and taught to set up spreadsheets, enter data, and create charts out of the data. The coaches were thus able to visually represent their progress.

Plan for a Sustainable Effort

Literacy coaching is a powerful vehicle for moving districts, buildings, and teachers toward their goals—you just want to make sure the vehicle doesn't run out of gas. Without plans in place to sustain the coaching effort, schools will implement ideas that may seem good at the time but do not make a difference in the long run (Fullan, 1985). The vehicle needs to keep moving regardless of staff turnover and the introduction of new goals.

Train the New Teachers

Because teachers who are in the district at the beginning of an initiative will receive more intensive training than newer ones, ongoing training is crucial for sustaining school improvement. When Maelou first began coaching teachers, she would grow impatient with novices who didn't seem to do anything she recommended. It eventually became obvious to her that most first-year teachers find it hard enough just trying to get from the opening bell to the closing bell, from Monday morning to Friday afternoon. A lot of what they do the first year is just for survival, so they should be treated gently—supported, encouraged, and given time to grow. A "new teacher day" can be held a few days before school resumes after a break or, in the case of year-round schools, at an appropriate time before the teacher starts in the classroom. In the case of a districtwide initiative, the literacy coach leadership team can facilitate new teacher training; for a school-level initiative, the school literacy coach and the principal can do so. When planning for a new teacher day, facilitators should

- Know how many new teachers will attend.
- Check the district schedule for conflicts.
- Secure the location and any audiovisuals needed.
- Train attendees in existing district or school initiatives (here's a good place to use those professional development videotapes).
- Provide handouts that explain the literacy initiative, along with any other relevant articles and books (the school or district may need to budget ahead of time for this).
- Explain the role of the literacy coach.
- Assemble materials such as curriculum guides that coaches will use in their teaching.
- Prepare to schedule additional coaching sessions among teachers and coaches at the meeting.

Once the initial training is completed, the new teachers will need "special handling" for the first year or, even better, the first two years. This is why ongoing coaching is important.

Remember Veteran Teachers

Coaching isn't just for new teachers. It's just as important for the veterans. Experience is a good thing, but it can also be a barrier. Experienced teachers need a special kind of approach that respects their knowledge and at the same time helps them integrate new learning into their practice.

One of the most successful methods in education is the Reading Recovery program (http://readingrecovery.org), which is specifically designed for 1st graders who are not making progress in reading. One of the primary reasons the program is such a success is that all Reading Recovery–trained teachers receive ongoing support and training. Even when content is repeated, teachers approach it with greater depth as they accrue greater knowledge and experience.

Think Ahead About Potential Problems

> *Expect the best, plan for the worst, and prepare to be surprised.*
>
> *—Denis Waitley*

It's always so much easier to get things right at the start than to try to fix them later. However, no matter how well you prepare, problems will arise, and you will need to solve them. Here are two common problems that we have encountered.

Problem #1: Nobody Is Using the Coach

Plan in advance to ensure that everyone will use a literacy coach, rather than waiting for teachers to request the coach's services. One way to do so is by requiring it in the district or school improvement plan. If any teachers manage to avoid working with the coach, the principal should nudge them to do so. Coaches can put monthly suggestions in teacher mailboxes, but we haven't found this to be very effective; posting a sign-up sheet for teachers is a better option (see Figure 1.4). In our experience, the most effective option of all is to seek out teachers throughout the day and bring up coaching during informal conversation.

Problem #2: Teachers Are Trying to Do It All

Sometimes teachers try to do everything themselves, resulting in a hodgepodge of practices, a confused vision, and an impossible schedule. Unless teachers get rid of outdated practices, they will be frustrated.

It is quite possible that a teacher may believe in outdated or even imagined requirements. For example, a kindergarten teacher may have the impression that the district requires 30 minutes of "calendar time" each morning, when no such requirement exists. Coaches and administrators should work together to clarify exactly what the current requirements are. The next and most essential step is to *communicate* those requirements to the teachers.

Summary

Now you know the fundamentals of preparing for a coaching initiative:

- Planning ahead so it will be sound from the beginning

FIGURE 1.4	Sample Sign-Up Sheet for Coaching Sessions

Literacy coach Amy Sandvold will be in the building on the following dates. Please write your name, a time, and what you would like her to model in the slots below using the following codes:

OB: Observation   IW: Interactive Writing   GR: Guided Reading

TGR: Transitional Guided Reading   MW: Making Words

COMP: Comprehension Strategies
(write which one)   _____

OTHER: (specify)   _____

Wed., April 10:   _____   _____
    _____   _____

Thurs., April 11:   _____   _____
    _____   _____

(Away April 15–19; see Gail Saunders-Smith)

Wed., April 24 *(afternoon; see Penny Beed in the morning):*
    _____   _____

(Away April 25)

Thurs., May 2:   _____   _____
    _____   _____

(Away May 8–9)

Wed., May 15:   _____   _____
    _____   _____

Thurs., May 16:   _____   _____
    _____   _____

- Making sure you do all you can do to make the effort sustainable
- Thinking ahead to better deal with potential problems

Having set the stage for coaching in your school, you're now ready for the next important step: making friends who can help coaching succeed.

Make Friends

Make new friends but keep the old.
Some are silver and the others gold.

—Old Girl Scout song

"Calling all coaches: we have a literacy emergency!"

Amy and her fellow coaches used to joke that they needed pagers to contact each other during literacy emergencies. Because coaching depends so much on communication with others, it is particularly important for coaches to build relationships and make friends in the school—indeed, in the whole school system.

Building Relationships

When Maelou was facilitating the Reading Excellence initiative, she spent hours on end putting together a teachers' handbook for the initiative with fellow coaches and key teachers. On the wall of the room hung a quote that read, "Success is what happens when preparation meets opportunity"—an adaptation of the Roman philosopher Seneca's quote, "Luck is what happens when preparation meets opportunity." By the time the Reading Excellence initiative came along, Maelou had worked in the district for several years and built relationships with others who, like her, were frustrated with the status quo, ready for change, and prepared in both attitude and knowledge to make change happen. Once the initiative was under way, it may have appeared to outsiders that those involved had accomplished a lot in a very short time—but much of that was only possible because they already knew "who their friends were," so they were prepared when the opportunity finally arrived!

Trust does not come in the benefit package along with insurance and a retirement account. Newly hired coaches have to build relationships with teachers over time, taking the initiative to work with them and to communicate their role in implementing the initiative. Teachers who become coaches in their schools may be viewed differently by their peers now that they're supposed to work with the teachers in their classrooms to improve teaching. In such cases, coaches might therefore feel uncomfortable and wonder how to maintain the teachers' trust. Cases where teachers are already close with their coaches are challenging as well, because coaches must prove that they can *still* be trusted.

Coaches who are completely new to their schools can feel overwhelmed when trying to connect with people they are meeting for the first time. They should keep in mind that the teachers feel the same way. The minute coaches are hired, administrators expect the teachers to work with them—they have invested money in on-site professional development, and they want results! Chances are slim to none that the teachers will greet the coaches with open arms, saying, "Oh, please, please, tell me how to do my job!"

The following are actual notes from a typical coaching day that Amy recorded in her notebook when she worked as a coach. You will notice how very important everyone in a school is to the success of a coach and to the effectiveness of an initiative. This example shows Amy communicating with the building secretary, the principal, the grant coordinator, the district office secretary, the media specialist, a special needs teacher, school associates, classroom teachers, fellow coaches, the school custodian, and students:

8:15–9:00
One teaching demonstration, one observation, and one individual student assessment today in classrooms. Check planner to see what rooms I'm in. Stop in office, drop off daily schedule, let secretary know I'm here today. Check with principal about next week's staff meeting agenda—we agree to add information about our upcoming professional development

visits. Bob needs new videotape for peer coaching videos, says one of the cameras is fuzzy or maybe tape is old. Constance wants handouts for next week's meeting, which she won't attend. She reviewed what I was going to observe in her classroom today. Touch base with special needs teacher, Helen, to discuss my teaching demonstration today. Quickly walk through my lesson with her and ask for suggestions.

9:00–9:50 (First period, no classroom work)

Check on videotape problem for Bob. Media specialist isn't in, so I get the key to camera room from custodian. Notice camera #3 is missing. Media specialist returns, doesn't know where missing camera is, gives me new tape for Bob. Put tape in Bob's mailbox. Discuss missing camera with principal.

9:50–10:30 (Individual student pullout)

Administer reading assessment to 3rd graders for state testing.

10:30–10:45 (First recess)

Ask school associates if they will print out district reading test results as promised—discuss how often and what computer to use. Give data to teachers. Work in time to discuss results at a future staff meeting? Call Maelou about missing camera, leave message with project secretary.

10:45–11:30 (Teaching demonstration in special needs classroom)

Model small-group transitional guided reading lesson with comprehension strategy of determining importance in nonfiction. Use book Creepy Crawlies *by Avelyn Davidson. Debrief lesson after school.*

11:30–12:20 (2nd grade classroom observation)

Watch Constance teach guided reading. Study skills focus on locating and using subheadings and tables of contents, finding key words, and summarizing. When students go to music, debrief lesson. Pick up students so that Constance can go to lunch early.

12:20–1:10 (Lunch)
Eat and talk with teachers in lounge; they are worried about how classes are distributed for next year. Lots of high-achieving kids—check on this. 5th grade teacher wants copy of fall writing samples back—has seen lots of growth, wants to compare. Ask teachers if I can photograph classrooms for district teacher guidebook. All say OK, so I ask them to write accompanying blurbs. Go get digital camera from media specialist.

1:10–2:30
Visit three rooms—Peg's, Ron's, and Mary Ann's. Take digital pictures of the word wall and interactive writing chart in 1st grade. Check with Bob; he got his tape.

2:30–2:45 (Recess)
John asks me to do a "Guess the Covered Word" demonstration next week. Will do it first thing on Wednesday morning. Call Maelou, who gives me the serial number for the missing camera.

2:45–3:20
Go to my desk in associates' room. Start typing up plan for upcoming professional development agenda.

3:20–4:05
Walk around and touch base with teachers. Debrief lesson with Helen from special needs room. Plan next sequence of coaching: me 5/9 (Wed.), Helen 5/10 (Thurs.), me 5/16 (Wed.), Helen 5/17 (Thurs.).

4:05–5:00 (Central office)
Check in with Maelou and other coaches. Discuss how to organize Dr.

Saunders-Smith's visit. Decide teachers need to give me questions to ask her by May 7th. Begin scheduling Dr. Saunders-Smith's classroom demonstrations.

Coaching Smart

Teachers need to know and trust that coaches know what they're doing, so coaches need to demonstrate their expertise. Consider the variety of literacy-related strategies and conversations that Amy engaged in according to the notes reprinted above: small-group reading demonstration in a classroom, individual student assessment, observation of small-group reading in a special needs classroom, planning for a demonstration of word work, and planning literacy professional development—all in just one day!

Although the International Reading Association cautions that "it is better to delay implementing a reading coaching initiative than to push ahead with inadequately trained reading coaches" (2004, p. 4), we would not recommend waiting around forever. Many teachers who find themselves thrust into coaching roles prematurely are still able to help teachers and their students. In an ideal world, all reading coaches would be highly qualified and well trained for the role, but sometimes on-the-job training is the only choice. Our advice for teachers who find themselves in this position is to call it an internship, then go for it!

Coaching with Heart

They may forget what you said, but they will never forget how you made them feel.

—Carl W. Buechner

You may have the IQ necessary to "coach smart," but do you have the EQ? Patti and Tobin (2003) coined the term *EQ* (short for "emotional quotient") to mean a measure of emotional intelligence. According to Goleman (1995), there are four general dimensions to emotional intelligence: self-awareness, self-management, social awareness, and relationship management.

Let's examine Amy's notes again, this time noting the many interactions that had more to do with emotions than with expertise or knowledge. What do you suppose staff members thought and felt when speaking with Amy? What did she think and feel? Let's reveal the hidden emotional side of Amy's day:

- When Amy met with the school secretary, do you think she began with a greeting or just slapped a note on her desk?
- Compare two ways in which Amy could have brought up the issue of the missing camera—"Someone stole the camera!" versus "I've noticed one of our cameras is missing. What do you think we should do about this?"
- Notice that Amy previews the lesson she is about to demonstrate for Helen and asks her for input. She doesn't just swoop down wearing her "expert" badge and do the lesson her way.
- Do you think Amy demanded immediate attention from the custodian, or do you think she approached him by saying, "When you have a moment, I need the key to the video equipment room"?

Choosing the positive approach in each of these interactions helps create a positive climate in the school. Teamwork is a defining principle of effective change (Hall & Hord, 2006), so it makes sense for coaches to build positive relationships with everyone. As

Barsade (2002) notes, positive energy is contagious: "People are 'walking mood inductors,' continuously influencing the moods and then the judgments and behaviors of others" (p. 667). How simple is that? Coaches who make up their minds to be positive can actually help those around them just by being in a good mood!

Whether students are doing well or poorly, teachers are always anxious for them to do better. It's the coach's job to stay positive in the face of others' high anxiety.

Putting Smart and Heart Together

The key in building productive relationships is to combine the intellectual and emotional aspects. As Patti and Tobin (2003) state, "The key to effective leadership and successful schools in the 21st century is good people, downright smart, caring people, who excel in both IQ and EQ" (p. 2). Once a balance of IQ and EQ is achieved, coaches need to persevere in relationship building to remain effective.

Who Are Your Friends?

Assuming that everyone is a friend is essential, but we all know that we build and maintain friendships differently with different people. Here are some specific "friends" with whom you must collaborate.

The Powers That Be

The partnership between principals and coaches is one of the most important indicators of how effective a coaching effort will be in a school. How principals present the coach's role from the very beginning will greatly affect teachers' receptiveness to coaching. It is critical for principals to serve as instructional leaders while coaches provide expertise and support: when principals monitor and evaluate teachers, coaches are free to support instruction.

Coaches should also make friends with district administrators, updating them on progress as often as possible. When administrators understand what's going on in a coaching initiative, they are much more likely to provide support when it is needed. Coaches should invite the district superintendent to observe professional development sessions in their buildings.

The *Really* Important People

Teachers are a coach's most important friends. They're both "customers" and resident experts. The biggest mistake coaches can make is to assume that they know everything and that teachers know nothing. Teachers have a lot to teach coaches, and the more they feel appreciated, the more they will trust in the coaching effort.

Communication is what holds friends together, and technology makes sharing your resident experts' ideas easy. Digital cameras and e-mail can be amazingly helpful when trying to share observations with other teachers. We used to take photos of classroom lessons in progress, add blurbs explaining the strategies pictured, and e-mail them to teachers across the district. In addition, Amy used to carry around one of those little fat memo pads; whenever she thought of something important, or whenever a teacher asked a question or shared an idea, she wrote it down. Coaches who think they're reading gods would insist on doing all the coaching themselves, but good coaches know better—they are well aware of their weaknesses and look to other teachers for expertise and ideas.

Writing follow-up notes after meetings, demonstrations, or observations is an excellent practice, but coaches must proceed with extreme caution: although it is important to thank teachers for their collaboration, the coaches don't want to be perceived as evaluating the teachers. Lieberman and Miller (1984) have found that all feedback, whether positive or negative, is counterproductive. Whether you agree with this or not, the point is to be careful. It's one thing to express appreciation and ask thought-provoking questions; it's quite another to make unsupported value judgments (e.g., "This is good" or "This is bad"). Here are examples of the types of phrases that coaches should use to help teachers feel safe and open to another round of coaching:

- Thank you for inviting me to visit your classroom today.
- I appreciated the opportunity to work with you and your students.
- I valued the time spent in your classroom.
- I look forward to working with you and your students again.
- I appreciated our time to collaborate today.

Your "Expert" Friends

Sometimes, your expert friends are right in the same district with you. When kindergarten teachers used to ask Amy about early childhood issues, for instance, she knew to consult her friends Barb, an innovative early literacy teacher, and Sylvia, the Title I early childhood consultant. Of course, coaches will sometimes need to reach outside of their districts to find experts in particular subjects. Don't be dazzled by big names: Dr. Literal may have an international reputation, but if he's all about phonics and you want your students to learn to *think,* his celebrity status means nothing. Here are some of the experts who were and continue to be more than friends to us.

Professional development providers. When we were working on the Reading Excellence initiative, Mary Ann Poparad, the Reading Recovery teacher leader, recommended that we enlist Gail Saunders-Smith to train our teachers in small-group reading instruction. Although we had heard of Gail, we had never seen her in action, but we trusted Mary Ann's expertise—and are we ever glad we did! Gail took us far beyond where we ever dreamed we could go. When another colleague recommended Angela Maiers as our "thinking" expert, we also accepted that recommendation— another brilliant bit of trust on our part! Angela taught our teachers and our students a whole new way of thinking about thinking.

Friends from higher education. Educators at colleges and universities are connected to the latest research and to the most distinguished experts. We highly recommend that you search out one or more of these higher ed friends as advisors.

One of our most valuable friends was Penny Beed, a professor from a nearby university. Penny had done a lot of work in our district, bringing her undergraduates into the schools to work with students. She was well known and trusted. We knew Penny personally and professionally and knew that she shared our philosophy and was wonderful to work with. Though down-to-earth and just plain nice, she is always mindful of maintaining a rigorous assessment–instruction cycle founded in research.

Penny provided professional development to the teachers. She advised us on how best to gather, organize, analyze, and use data. She advised us on instructional matters. She was, in other words, the coaches' coach.

Language arts coordinators. Knowledgeable, agreeable language arts coordinators can be some of your very best friends. Really paying attention to their advice and keeping them in the loop not only will tap into their expertise but will also keep everyone happier.

Special teachers. Title I teachers, reading teachers, and special needs teachers can be valued as professionals by a school, or they can be turned into Cinderellas, doing all the work nobody else wants to do but getting none of the credit. You will do well to treat special teachers as resident experts—they have expertise and knowledge that can be of great benefit to a coaching effort.

Technical support staff. Being in charge of the technical stuff, like videotaping, can be pretty challenging. One of our colleagues, "Dan, the Video Man," used to have to carry a heavy camera and tripod up and down stairs, sometimes with a bad back; wait around when somebody messed up the schedule; stand behind the camera for hours on end; and make endless copies of each lesson to distribute to the individual schools. Yet through it all, Dan remained cheerful and cooperative, going out of his way to do a good job. This may simply have been his personality, but we like to think it's because he was treated with respect and affection. He became our friend, not just a district employee doing his job.

School secretaries. No matter what anyone tells you, most building secretaries are in charge! The secret to making friends with school secretaries is to communicate daily to them where you will be and when. A simple message on a sticky note will work, but if you are organized, you may want to develop a schedule sheet and make additional copies for yourself and the principal. If money is not an obstacle, then pagers are another good way to ensure you can be found to receive a call.

Custodians. If custodians only did what was listed in their job descriptions, a lot of important things wouldn't get done. There's usually a lot of setting up to do for professional development; without a custodian friend, you may have to spend precious time moving furniture around instead of coaching.

The Rest (Friends-in-Waiting)

He drew a circle that shut me out—
Heretic, rebel, a thing to flout.
But love and I had the wit to win:
We drew a circle that took him in.

—*Edwin Markham*

You know exactly the people we're talking about: the resisters who make it clear that they do not agree with you, they will not change, and what's more, they will go out of their way to make things difficult for you. They dream up various excuses for themselves: "I only have two years left before retirement." "Scores are good, so why change now?" "Scores are so bad there's no hope of changing them." "I teach math (or science or social studies), not reading!" Others believe that coaching is pure nonsense and not worth the time, or that it won't work with "our kids." So what can you do while you're waiting for these friends-in-waiting to become full-fledged friends? Here are a few ideas.

Just be nice—and keep moving. The resisters' excuses are many and complicated, but how you handle them is simple: you have to be a velvet steamroller, advancing determinedly but gently. You want everyone to see that you cannot be deterred or undermined by a few dissenters, but you also want to leave the dissenters their dignity. Remember, you don't want to give up on them, ever!

When handling difficult situations, our core philosophy is to keep on being nice, keep on trying, and smile a lot. (It also helps to bring lots of chocolate!) If we fail to do these things, we become disconnected from resisters, and it becomes very difficult to build up relationships again.

Be a friend. It's not easy to be a friend to someone who is anything but a friend to you, but the moment you start treating dissenters like enemies is the moment you begin losing the chance to win them over. Sometimes you need to practice unilateral friendship.

Think of how you treat your personal friends: you take an interest in them. You're nice to them. Above all, you don't talk about them behind their backs. It's so easy to get caught in the web of negativity, especially in the teachers' lounge—a dangerous place, the teachers' lounge! Someone starts talking about the dissenters, it turns negative, and before you know it, you're going along. There is a lot of social pressure to agree with negative comments from those who are on your side. You have to catch yourself and stay positive.

Keep everyone connected. While you're waiting for "the rest" to come around, keep working to build a literacy community that includes them. Changing environments changes your thinking.

In a relaxed, social state of mind, you can apply and synthesize what you have been doing and make plans for what you're going to do next.

Amy recalls being shocked after helping to facilitate a literacy workshop in one Iowa school district: the sessions were packed with preK–12 staff, even though attendance was voluntary. The superintendent and most principals attended every single day, sitting right with everybody else. One evening, the superintendent reserved a room at a local restaurant for teachers to mingle and socialize over chips, salsa, and beverages. Although most of the talk was about summer plans, some discussion of work also took place. After speaking with the superintendent, it became clear to Amy that the leaders in this district were committed to building relationships and providing opportunities outside of the school to connect. We know the importance of in-the-workplace professional development, but out-of-the-workplace opportunities also help build and maintain connections among colleagues.

When resisters eventually decide to be friends, it is tempting to say, "It's about time!" or worse yet, "You expect me to go back and coach you through all of that stuff we have already done?" Our frustrations with former resisters can surface in our behaviors as well, such as when we hesitate to share what we know with them or to invite them to meetings. We must work hard to treat all staff as if they were on board all along.

Let's say that for the past year you have been coaching a team of teachers in comprehension strategies. Mr. Resister, a 20-year veteran, has not participated in any of the training or study groups or taken the opportunity to work with you as a coach. Now, for some reason, he is ready to try out some of the comprehension strategies. He wants you to plan with him and do a teaching demonstration in his classroom.

How do you treat Mr. Resister's new interest? You can be skeptical and wonder if he wants an hour to sit at the back of his room while you teach his students, or you can trust that he is sincere. No matter what his reason is for wanting you to work with him, you still have the chance to build a relationship and truly move forward together when you trust that he is sincere.

Some teachers will do what you want them to without believing that it's right or sharing your beliefs. Take what you can get: first focus on behavior, then focus on beliefs. Let resisters know that you respect their beliefs, then sit back. Some will see for themselves that what you're promoting makes sense—belief will follow behavior.

Summary

Making friends is the right thing to do. The guidelines we've laid out in this chapter will help you treat people the way you would like to be treated. Teachers will be more cooperative and more accepting. Your learning community will be a happy place in which to work, and you will be a happy literacy coach!

Teach!

I am always ready to learn, although I do not always like being taught.

—Winston Churchill

No matter the age, subject matter, setting, or goal, a learner is always a learner. Literacy coaches are teachers, and like the very best teachers, they not only *present* their learners with new information but also use the fundamentals of good teaching to support them as they learn, practice, and integrate new learning into their teaching.

Too often, administrators hear of a new practice and either dispatch teachers to learn about it or arrange for professional development a few times during the year. The teachers get overwhelmed, and the administrators end up disappointed with the teachers' implementation—"They were taught it, so why aren't they able to do it?"

Literacy coaching provides the scaffolding that typical professional development cannot, as coaches gradually release responsibility to the learner while providing ongoing support. In coaching, as in teaching of any kind, it is crucial to use your resources, apply what you know, understand the difference between knowing and doing, and most of all, remember that you are teaching people, not programming computers.

Characteristics of Adult Learners

According to Malcolm Knowles (1990), six characteristics distinguish adult learners from children:

1. The need to know. Adults are relevancy oriented: they need to know not only the goal but also why it's important. Part of your job as a literacy coach is to clarify goals.

2. Self-conception. Adults are autonomous and self-directed: they are reluctant to turn any control over to even the most knowledgeable authority.

3. The role of experience. Adults have accumulated a foundation of life experiences and knowledge from which they will instinctively draw, including work, family, and prior education.

4. Readiness to learn. Because of their experiences, adults are better prepared to learn what they need to know to be more effective in their real-life situations. Unlike younger learners, they can clearly see the application of learning.

5. Orientation to learning. Adults are practical: they want to focus on the skills and knowledge that are most useful to them and may not be interested in the underlying theories. A pinch of theory per pound of practice should be enough, though you should always be ready to supply more to those who want or need it.

6. Motivation. Adults are responsive to external motivators such as better jobs or higher salaries, but they are also internally motivated—they know and appreciate the joy of feeling that they are doing a good job.

We have found that there's an additional and not entirely positive characteristic of adult learners that Knowles doesn't mention. In our experience, some adults seem to think that they've spent a long time working things out and that their education is complete. We have found that it can be hard to convince teachers of the idea that very few things are learned all at one time. Reading, for example, is a continually developing process that we will all still be learning more about throughout our lives.

Here's an example. At one of the districts in which we worked, one particular (and excellent) professional developer came many times to teach us about small-group reading instruction. The first few times she presented, she used the same handout. Some of the teachers were outraged: "We already learned this! Didn't she even bother to make a new handout? How much are we paying her?" As the professional developer explained, the workshop wasn't about the handout. It was about the discussion and presentation, which took us deeper and deeper into understanding. Teachers were required to assume an active role that they had not been accustomed to in their usual "sit-and-get" in-service trainings. They had to take responsibility for their own learning.

Getting teachers to think about learning as a continual process should start at the outset. At the beginning of an initiative, bring out the analogies. Remind teachers of their own attempts to get really good at playing golf, making a cake, or driving a car. Talk about what they have observed in their students' learning—how it gets higher, wider, and deeper with each exposure to information. If teachers start to grumble later on, remind them of this initial discussion.

The Literacy Coach as Teacher

Although adults may differ from younger learners in some ways, they are the same in most. Below are some basic principles that apply to teaching adult learners as much as to younger ones.

Know Your Resources

The richest people can lead the poorest lives if they leave all of their money under the mattress. Here are some important resources you should consider tapping into when gearing up to coach.

Yourself. We sometimes fail to remind ourselves that if we find particular learning methods to be most effective, others will have their own set of preferences as well. For example, Maelou is aware that she learns best when the same information is presented to her in a variety of ways, but especially when it is written. She also knows that when she gets in over her head, she stops learning. For her part, Amy is a research enthusiast—she just loves reading it! Of course, not everyone is interested in learning this way, as her teaching partners have reminded her over the years ("Amy, you don't have a life, do you?"). Knowing this makes Amy careful not to start every sentence with "Research says. . . ." Amy also has to be social in order to learn: she needs time to talk to people about their perspectives before focusing on what she is going to do herself. (Costa and Garmston's 1994 book *Cognitive Coaching: A Foundation for Renaissance Schools* includes a valuable exercise that you can use to identify your own underlying belief system and cognitive style.)

Your "real" students. Most literacy coaches are teachers, and as teachers we constantly analyze our students' learning and our methods of teaching. Yet somehow, when the task shifts to teaching adults, we fail to apply what we learn from our "real" (i.e., younger) students. We forget, for example, that covering curriculum doesn't equal teaching.

Your "co-conspirators." You may have at one time belonged to the "closed-door" school of teaching, where teachers close their doors and do their own thing without sharing information with peers—either because someone might steal your good ideas or because someone might find out that you have no idea what you're doing! Coaching is definitely not the time to close the door. You can't do it alone. If there are other literacy coaches in the district, they can be your support team, but members of your team don't all have to have the same job title as you. All they need is the interest and the desire to make literacy coaching work.

The literature. A lot of people have spent a lot of time discovering what makes for effective teaching and learning, and it would be ridiculous to ignore all of that expertise. The trick is to combine what you learn from the literature with your experience, the context, and your own common sense. For example, let's say a district mandates a schoolwide initiative requiring that reciprocal teaching be used in all classrooms. The literature suggests that reciprocal teaching should be encouraged (Raphael, 1984). Does this mean that reciprocal teaching should be used in every single class, including volleyball? Clearly, this is one of those times when the principal needs to rely more on common sense than on the mandate.

Teach from the Known to the New

When we first begin to teach students a new concept, we usually use some kind of analogy—we try to help them see how the "new" information is similar to something that they already know. For example, if you want students to get the idea of how events are sequenced, you may discuss a familiar process such as brushing teeth. Analogies serve as mental anchors, and adults need them as much as younger students do.

Both of our primary professional developers for the Reading Excellence initiative were masters of providing mental anchors for adult learners. Although very different in personality, they could expertly teach adults complex concepts through analogies and clear, simple language. Coaching is certainly easier when it follows adult learner–friendly professional development and can meet teachers where they are. For example, when we trained teachers in the comprehension strategy of questioning, it became evident that many teachers still believed questioning should take place at the end of reading. By validating the teachers' belief in the power of questioning and coaching them in the research on questioning as an active process that occurs before, during, and after reading, we were able to nudge them toward more effective instruction.

Teachers are often in a state of self-induced frustration. It is the coach's job to convince them that they are OK, that they know more than they think they do. The more the coach can convince teachers that they do not have to replace what they have already been doing with all-new instructional practices, the more productive coaching will be.

Gradual Release of Responsibility

Classroom teaching is not unlike teaching a child to ride a bike: both are gradual processes that provide support and result in the learner's ability to go whizzing off on his own. In education, of course, support is called scaffolding and serves as a powerful tool for helping learners become independent (Beed, Hawkins, & Roller, 1991).

Pearson and Gallagher (1983) use the term "gradual release of responsibility." Notice in Figure 3.1 that learning increases as the learner gains responsibility.

Consider the following example: Mr. Eager, a third-year 3rd grade teacher, has been selected at random by his district to attend the International Reading Association (IRA) Conference, held every spring in some tourist-friendly city and attended by thousands of teachers. He has picked up his official name badge and his packet of materials and is sitting on a sofa in the hall of the convention center, trying to choose the sessions he will attend. He knows that his district is planning to implement Taffy Raphael's Question-

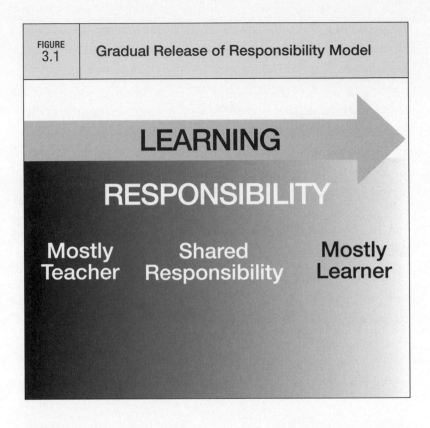

FIGURE 3.1 Gradual Release of Responsibility Model

LEARNING

RESPONSIBILITY

Mostly Teacher   Shared Responsibility   Mostly Learner

Answer-Response (QAR) Strategy (Raphael, 1984) because it has been given the blessing of the No Child Left Behind Act.

Mr. Eager sees that Dr. Masters of Prestige University is going to be doing a QAR presentation at 2:00 in Ballroom A. Great! He'll have a head start on his colleagues! So Mr. Eager attends the session, is lucky enough to get a handout before they're all gone, and sits through a very impressive PowerPoint presentation loaded with statistics presented in all kinds of colorful graphics. As he leaves, he throws the handout in his briefcase and heads for the next session. He doesn't have time to think about what he's heard; he just wants to get a good seat for the session on writing in science class.

When he gets back to school, Mr. Eager is consumed with end-of-year duties. He carefully places all of his conference notes and handouts in a folder marked "IRA Conference," which he files in one of the boxes he plans to take home for the summer. Over the summer he takes two classes to keep his certificate current, so he never gets to the bottom of the box where the QAR handout is. Two weeks before school starts, he empties the box and organizes the contents to be taken back to school. During workshop week, he finds that a mandatory session for all K–6 teachers is on QAR—taught by, of all people, Dr. Masters from Prestige University! Mr. Eager is delighted because he's sure that now Dr. Masters will show him how to really *do* QAR.

Wrong! Out comes the PowerPoint, and Dr. Masters presents exactly the same theoretical information as she did at the conference. After the presentation, Mr. Topp, principal of Mr. Eager's school, has about 10 minutes to meet with his teachers. He tells them that they will need to start implementing QAR with their students by September 15. He wants to be reasonable, so he tells them he believes that delaying implementation until the middle of the month will give them enough time to get their seating charts made, their discipline under control, and the start-of-the-year testing done.

If we apply the above example to the diagram in Figure 3.1, Mr. Eager has found himself in the "Mostly Teacher" area twice: once at the IRA conference and once at the district workshop. He is now being asked, without any real instruction and certainly without any modeling, to enter the "Mostly Learner" area with no support, where he, as the learner turned magically to teacher, will begin teaching his students to use the QAR strategy. This scenario is illustrated in Figure 3.2.

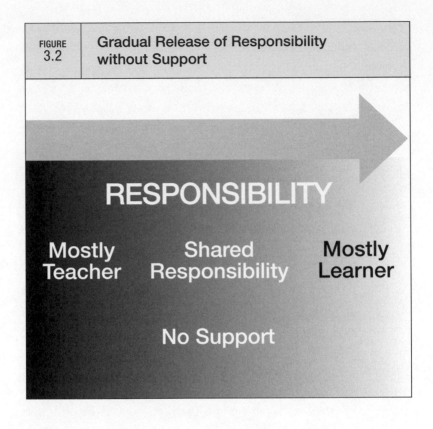

FIGURE 3.2	Gradual Release of Responsibility without Support

RESPONSIBILITY

Mostly Teacher Shared Responsibility Mostly Learner

No Support

For Mr. Eager, the "Mostly Learner" area may as well be rechristened "You're on Your Own." He is not at all ready to apply what little he's learned, and there appears to be no plan in place to support him as he bumbles through.

Now let's look at what might have been. Figure 3.3 incorporates examples from a well-designed coaching sequence into the scaffolding model. Note that learning continues through the "Mostly Teacher" area, the "Shared Responsibility" area, and the "Mostly Learner" area.

FIGURE 3.3	Gradual Release of Responsibility with Support

LEARNING

RESPONSIBILITY

| Mostly Teacher | Shared Responsibility | Mostly Learner |

- Monitoring
- Reflection
- Independent Practice
- Guided Practice
- Scaffolding
- Peer Coaching

Mr. Eager's example highlights a common mistake in coaching: a lack of scaffolding or guided instruction. If Mr. Eager had been appropriately supported, his experience would have been much different. It would begin the same way, with Dr. Masters's presentation at IRA. In this case, however, Mr. Facilitate, a literacy coach from Mr. Eager's school, would attend the same presentation and would *not* invite Dr. Masters to the district for workshop week. Instead, he would collaborate with co-conspirators (his fellow coaches and the district language arts coordinator) to arrange a series of QAR sessions, starting during workshop week but continuing once a month throughout the year. They would plan the sessions carefully, starting with a simple model of QAR and adding a new layer of complexity with each subsequent session. Between sessions, coaches would model in classrooms and teachers would meet to discuss their use of QAR.

As the year progressed and the teachers' expertise grew, coaches would begin to observe teachers using QAR in their classrooms and teachers would begin to engage in peer coaching. Principals would encourage teachers to implement QAR slowly with their students and make it clear that quality of implementation would not be evaluated just yet. At this point, collaboration and coaching would be the focus. The process would continue until all teachers were comfortable with QAR and could teach it to their students (using scaffolding, of course).

Zone of Proximal Development

Vygotsky (1978) labeled the difference between what learners can do with help and what they can do independently the Zone of Proximal Development (ZPD). In this zone, learners are challenged enough to keep learning but supported enough to feel secure. Coaches should strive to identify teachers' ZPDs at any given moment and adjust their coaching accordingly, allowing each teacher to work within his or her individual ZPD.

Madeline Hunter's Instructional Sequence

Madeline Hunter's instructional sequence is the practical application of the gradual release of responsibility model (Hunter, 1986). In its original form, it has the following seven components:

1. **Objectives** (what you want the student to be able to learn and do)

2. **Standards** (what the students will be able to do)
3. **Anticipatory Set** (the "hook"—how new learning relates to what learners already know)
4. **Teaching** (including input, modeling, and the ever-popular checking for understanding)
5. **Guided Practice/Monitoring** (putting new learning into practice with teacher support)
6. **Closure** (review and summary of the learning)
7. **Independent Practice** (putting new learning into practice without teacher support, but under supervision)

An important eighth step—application—is not included in Hunter's original model; teachers have only limited control over it. If there is no application, there is no point to the learning except as an intellectual exercise. Worse yet is faulty application, which can be a consequence of poor or nonexistent scaffolding.

Differentiated Learning

In the words of Thomas Jefferson, "There is nothing more unequal than the equal treatment of unequal people." When at all possible, provide learning opportunities that meet the individual needs of individuals by making information available in multiple formats. Different students learn in different ways: some do better individually, others do better in groups; some prefer reading or listening, others prefer viewing graphics or touching or manipulating objects.

The Difference Between Teaching and Learning

It is one thing for a teacher to follow the curriculum, finish the book, or remain on schedule; it is quite another to ensure that students have actually learned. Your job as a coach is not to teach, but *to see that your learners learn*. This isn't as easy to monitor with adults as it is with younger learners; you can't administer a post-test or observe the teachers daily in a self-contained class-room. Monitoring adult learning requires that you be creative and thoughtful, not to mention tireless. As a coach, much of what you are able to find out about your learners' learning will be anecdotal and will come from teacher logs, discussions of study groups, and even private conversations with teachers. You have to pay attention, keep good notes, look for patterns, and draw conclusions from your data.

The Difference Between Learning and Doing

Let's assume that most of your teachers have learned what it is you want them to learn. Remember that even though they have learned *how* to do, they are not *doing*—when they are not being monitored, they slip back into their old practices.

As Maelou's son Jeff once put it, "Anything I've ever done wrong wasn't because I didn't know better." Very often in life we know what we're supposed to do, and we know how to do what we're supposed to do, but for a million different reasons, we just don't do it! Why does this happen? Why don't teachers use what they have learned to help their students? There probably aren't a *million* different reasons, but there are a lot. Here are a few:

- Teachers tend to teach the way they were taught. That's just human nature. In a strange sort of way it's encouraging, because it means that teaching works!
- Remember that whenever a new practice is introduced, chances are good that it will be replacing an old one—and sometimes teachers need both clarification and permission to "weed the garden" of outdated, ineffective practices.
- Teachers may not have had enough experience with the new technique for it to become habitual. Like learning a foreign language, learning a new technique can be tiring.

- It's not the teachers' idea, it's a top-down mandate. Richardson (2003) argues that teachers change all of the time when it's their own idea to do so. Let's try meeting Richardson's challenge "to operate within this naturalistic sense of teacher change. Since teachers change all the time, a strategy here would be to determine the ways in which they make their decisions to change and provide input and help when they do so" (p. 403).

Remember "the Person"

Amy remembers clearly a moment when she forgot "the person." She was coaching a group of teachers in small-group reading instruction and thought it would be a good idea to create implementation logs tailored to each teacher's level of progress.

One of her younger colleagues was mortified. How embarrassing it would be to turn in a log showing her to be in the beginning levels of implementation!

Amy had forgotten the person. Often, in our obsession with results, we lose sight of what the teachers feel. If we forget about the person behind the student (in this case, the teacher), we become top-down coaches, making people do what we think they should do rather than meeting them where they are.

Summary

We hope you have not been insulted by our overview of the fundamentals of teaching, but we were willing to take that risk, because if coaching is not guided by the principles of teaching and learning, the results will be as poor as those in a 2nd grade class under haphazard instruction. Learning in any context is only ever as good as the instruction behind it.

Be Consistent

A consistent man believes in destiny, a capricious man in chance.

—Benjamin Disraeli

In order to do their very best work, coaches must be consistent. Consistent coaching results in strong learning with good application, a sense of community among teachers, and (most important) increased student achievement. By contrast, when coaching is inconsistent, teachers feel insecure and demoralized because they are never sure what they are supposed to be doing. They are in a constant state of relearning or correcting their learning, or very possibly giving up on even trying to learn because it's all too confusing. Morale is low, and people are unable to do their very best work. Students feel the effects of their teachers' confusion, and this in turn affects *their* ability to excel in the classroom.

Consistency of Purpose and Vision

Coaches are hired for a very specific purpose: to increase teacher expertise by providing ongoing, in-the-workplace professional development that will, in turn, directly affect student learning. Though strategies may vary, the purpose of coaching remains the same. According to Schmoker (2002), "the key" to consistency (which he calls "regularity") "is to regularly marshal collective intelligence and chart progress toward goals that teachers have agreed upon" (p. 63). What better way to follow his advice than to keep your goals simple and attainable and then work toward them consistently? Having consistent goals and vision allows you to set priorities and sets the stage for an organized coaching initiative because you are able to focus on what is important.

Consistency of Organization

People deal with the frustration caused by disorganization in different ways, most of which are not very productive. Literacy coaches should do their very best to spare the teachers and themselves that frustration. Being involved in a new and intense initiative is stressful enough without the added frustration of disorganization.

Consistency in Attitude

Consider the following example. Most mornings, Ms. Educate is at the door of her 2nd grade classroom to greet all students individually and wish them a good day. This morning, however, she woke up late, got a flat tire on the way to work, and came into her classroom feeling totally unprepared. She just doesn't have time to greet her students because she's busy organizing the guided reading schedule for the day. The students sense that something is wrong. Their insecurity is such that they begin to bicker and wander around the room, until soon there is chaos. Ms. Educate and the students leave that afternoon with a vague feeling of having had a day that was not quite right.

You've seen it happen, not just in classrooms but also in offices and at meetings. The usually positive, cheerful leader is not her usual self, so the day feels a little off for everyone. Without a consistently positive attitude, you too can have that effect—not just on a single day but on an entire coaching initiative.

Although you must be cheerful and positive, you must also be sympathetic toward others' frustrations. Maelou had a wonderful former boss, Dorothy, whose attitude was perfect. When one of her employees would start to whine, she would simply say, calmly and sympathetically, "I know. I know." It wasn't *what* she said but the way she said it—in a voice full of understanding, but one that also conveyed the message that we have to get on with the work at hand.

This attitude must be consistent from day to day, from month to month, from situation to situation, and most of all, from person to person. You are the one who is setting the mood. You are the one who believes the work can be done. It's an awesome responsibility, and more than a bit of a stretch at times, but it also grants you great power—the power to fulfill the vision and the purpose of the initiative.

Consistency in the Coaching Model

Whether you follow an established coaching model or decide to design your own, you need to ask yourself whether it matches your purpose and vision and whether it's effective. The model you select should reflect the concepts of teaching for effective learning, including gradual release of responsibility. Once you have carefully selected a coaching model, stick with it!

Peer Coaching

There are different perspectives on how much teachers should know about a new strategy before they begin coaching each other. Some believe that teacher expertise increases even when the teachers have limited knowledge and proficiency; others believe that only expert coaching is effective. We stand somewhere in the middle. Peer coaching is extremely powerful. There is a dramatic difference in results between professional development in which teachers only receive information (e.g., from a lecture or a video) and professional development that includes theory, demonstration, practice, and peer coaching. If you as a literacy coach can be there to provide support and help gauge teachers' level of expertise, then peer coaching can be effective. As Schmoker notes, "Regular monitoring, followed by adjustment, is the only way to expect success" (1996, p. 5).

The Increasing Teacher Expertise Coaching Model

When we worked on the Reading Excellence initiative together, we struggled to provide the appropriate degree of scaffolding given the scope of the initiative and the ratio of coaches to teachers at the school. Our solution was to devise the Increasing Teacher Expertise (ITE) coaching model (see Figure 4.1). We wanted a model that would increase the amount of practice teachers had with new strategies, would fit within the regular school day with the least amount of interruption possible, and would not require substitute teachers for in-class peer coaching.

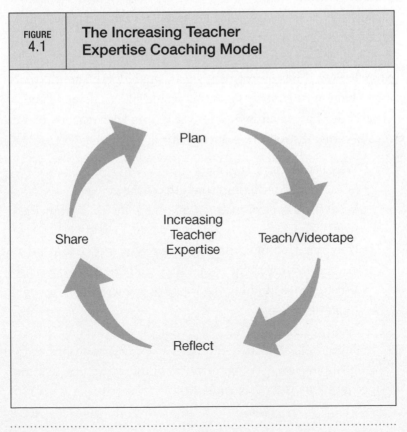

FIGURE 4.1	The Increasing Teacher Expertise Coaching Model

Plan

Increasing Teacher Expertise

Teach/Videotape

Reflect

Share

We based the ITE model on the research of Joyce and Showers (1995) as well as on Fenstermacher's (1993) "Practical Argument" model, which has also been used by coaches working with graduate and undergraduate students in the University of Northern Iowa Reading Clinic for Children (Tidwell, Hoewing, & Ko-Bras, 2003). In the ITE model, all teachers have the opportunity to reflect, self-evaluate, problem solve, and synthesize data, either individually with a coach or in coaching teams made up of grade-level colleagues.

The ITE model cycle involves an ongoing flow of planning, teaching/videotaping, reflecting, and sharing. Here is an example of how the cycle would work for teachers learning about small-group reading instruction.

Step 1: Plan. The coach works with a grade-level team of teachers to plan what strategy he or she would like to demonstrate or observe during a small-group reading lesson. Each teacher focuses on answering the following questions:

- Why is this group together?
- What are the needs and strengths of the group?
- What is the next instructional step for this group, and why?
- How am I doing with prompting students to use newly learned strategies when what they read doesn't make sense?
- What change am I hoping to see in my teaching? How will I know if it happens?

A small-group lesson plan template can provide a record of the lesson planning. Supporting members of the group may ask clarifying questions, but they must be careful not to be critical or evaluative. Colleagues may respond to a teacher's specific request for input on instruction.

Step 2: Teach/Videotape. This step occurs during the instructional day and may occur several days after the planning session. If the coach is observing, teachers implement the strategy discussed in Step 1 in front of their students, preferably videotaping themselves at the same time. (If the coach is demonstrating a strategy, a videotape is not made.) The coach will meet with the teachers at a later time to reflect, possibly after school or during an early dismissal day.

In addition to conducting live demonstrations of strategies, consider showing videotapes of other teachers, coaches, or professional developers to teachers or having them role-play (e.g., by acting as students while one of them conducts a demonstration).

Step 3: Reflect. If teachers were videotaped in Step 2, each one should then view his or her video and select a brief segment (five minutes at the longest) on which to reflect by answering the following three questions:

1. Step by step, describe what's taking place in this segment. (*Sample answer:* I say to the students, "You know about accidents," which is what the book is about. Then I do "the picture walk.")
2. In a nutshell, state what these actions represent. (*Sample answer:* I am making a coaching statement to get the students to think of what they know about accidents.)
3. Why am I doing what I'm doing in the video? (*Sample answer:* Research shows the importance of calling up background knowledge to support successful reading.)

Step 4: Share. This step takes place during early dismissal or common planning time or after school. The grade-level team reconvenes, and teachers share their selected segments and written reflections with their peers. During this sharing time, colleagues must be careful not to make evaluative comments (though they may thank the presenting teacher and comment generally that they've learned something useful). If time permits, teachers may begin planning the next lesson. The coach should reflect on this cycle by answering the questions in Step 3.

Consistency in Scheduling

Figure 4.2 shows a sample schedule for grade-level team coaching based on the ITE model cycle.

FIGURE 4.2	Sample Schedule for Grade-Level Team Coaching		
Round 1			
Step	Group A: K–1	Group B: 2–3	Group C: 4–5
Plan	February 28	March 7	March 21
Videotape/ Reflect	March 1–9	March 8–April 3	March 22–April 3
Share	March 21	April 4	April 4
Round 2			
Step	Group A: K–1	Group B: 2–3	Group C: 4–5
Plan	April 4	April 18	April 18
Videotape/ Reflect	April 5–17	April 19–27	April 19–27
Share	April 18	May 2	May 2

When working as a coach in the Reading Excellence schools in Waterloo, Amy, along with Carol, the other reading coach, decided to create a schedule of what teachers would be doing and when. Teachers had to share the video equipment, so not all of them could be in the same place in the cycle at the same time. We've included the schedule we came up with for the months of April and May in Figure 4.3.

You can save teachers and administrators a lot of time by designing a simple schedule of rounds or cycles of grade-level team coaching. For example, during Round 1 in the schedule in Figure 4.2, Group A will be using the video equipment and going through the coaching cycle from February 28 to March 21; Group B, from March 7 to April 4; and Group C, from March 21 to April 4. The chart can easily be adapted depending on how much video equipment a building has and the pace at which you'd like to conduct the coaching.

For one week each month, teachers should record how many times they have taught a newly learned strategy in their classrooms until the optimal number of practices has been met; Carran (2000) suggests that 15 to 20 times is optimal. Because it's sometimes difficult for teachers to see that they're not just doing the same thing over and over for the sake of compliance, it is helpful to establish some benchmarks that show teachers that they're improving. Teachers should be looking for changes in their students as well as in themselves; after all, no matter how perfectly a lesson is taught, if the students don't learn, it's just another song and dance. Sometimes, improvements are simply changes in student attitude. During the Reading Excellence initiative, we would often ask teachers to write down the changes they saw in their students, so that they could see for themselves that they were making progress. Occasionally,

FIGURE 4.3 Sample Schedule for Peer Coaching

Date (Mondays)	Cycle A Grade ___	Cycle B Grade ___	Cycle C Grade ___	Cycle D Grade ___	Cycle E Grade ___
April 1	Plan and tape	MT 8 & STW 8	Analyze GSS tape for Teacher Talk	MT 8 & STW 8	Analyze GSS tape for Teacher Talk
April 8	View and reflect	Plan and tape	MT 8 & STW 8	Analyze GSS tape for Teacher Talk	MT 8 & STW 8
April 22	Share tape (5 min.)	View and reflect	Plan and tape	MT 9 & STW 10	On your own
April 29	MT 8 & STW 8	Share tape (5 min.)	View and reflect	Plan and tape	MT 9 & STW 10
May 6	Analyze GSS tape for Teacher Talk	MT 9 & STW 10	Share tape (5 min.)	View and reflect	Plan and tape
May 13	MT 9 & STW 10	Analyze GSS tape for Teacher Talk	MT 9 & STW 10	Share tape (5 min.)	View and reflect
May 20	On your own	On your own	On your own	On your own	Share tape (5 min.)

Key:
GSS = Gail Saunders-Smith
MT = *Mosaic of Thought*
STW = *Strategies That Work*

Please hand your written reflection in to Amy Sandvold after you show your tape. When analyzing the GSS tape for Teacher Talk, please use the "coaching for metacognition and inquiry" sheet.

Agenda:
1. Calendar: GSS here for the last time on Monday, April 15 (please write down a first and second choice for times); Angela Maiers here on Tuesday, May 14, and after school that day
2. Implementation logs: April 1–5
3. Reflection logs: April 8–12, plus one more during peer coaching
4. Peer coaching: Sign up for one peer coaching cycle. Two grades will have to sign up for the same cycle (some juggling of cameras will need to be organized).

teachers would spontaneously report successes—such as the veteran 5th grade teacher who marveled, "My kids are always asking me when they get to have their group. They actually like it!"

Consistency in Paperwork

Sometimes changing forms is necessary, but sometimes it offers no improvement at all. Our advice is to design forms carefully from the beginning and then think long and hard before you tweak them. If it isn't broken, leave it alone!

It is also a good idea to have a lesson plan for coaching, using the same steps as in the school or district's chosen coaching model, as these can be valuable as implementation guides. Devising a system for filing these plans, such as by maintaining a separate binder for each school with edge tabs for grade levels, will save time later when you are asked to demonstrate one of the lessons again. Just figure out what works and stick with it. The same applies to logs and other data-collection forms: design them carefully, keeping in mind what you want to learn from them and how you will organize and analyze the data. Then, leave them alone!

Full-Time Coaching

In terms of consistency, the ideal configuration is to have a full-time literacy coach who works only in one building, working with a single school staff, providing on-site coaching on consecutive days. In such a scenario, the coach can really get to know the teachers, students, and culture of the school, making the coaching more personal and effective.

If a coach must serve more than one building, we recommend limiting it to no more than two schools; otherwise, scheduling back-to-back coaching days is almost impossible, and staying consistent becomes more and more difficult. Figure 4.4 shows a sample week's schedule for a coach working at two schools.

FIGURE 4.4	Sample Week's Schedule for Coaching at Two Schools			
Monday	Tuesday	Wednesday	Thursday	Friday
Building A	Building A	Building A first 9 weeks; coaches' meeting in p.m.	Building B	Building B

Many districts are working more and more professional development time into the week during early dismissal days. If there isn't an early dismissal day in your district, consider holding coaching meetings on Friday afternoons. (If you are working at two schools, you may want to spend Friday mornings at one school for the first nine weeks and then switch.)

Combining the Roles of Literacy Coach and Reading Teacher

Being consistent in a combined role requires special dedication and creativity. Some literacy coaches split their day between coaching and another role, such as reading teacher; others coach before and after the regular school day.

Amy was once specifically hired to serve both as a coach to teachers and as a full-time reading teacher to children. The district was providing training in guided reading and reciprocal teaching, and the school set every Thursday afternoon aside for teacher collaboration, so the vision (providing quality reading instruction) was in place at the district level, and the purpose (making the instruction work) was in place at the school level.

Although she was hired in part to coach teachers, Amy found that she spent most of her time working with pullout groups of struggling students and teaching guided reading with the 1st grade teachers; there was no teacher coaching in classrooms. Although she might occasionally speak at a staff meeting or deliver a Power-Point presentation on comprehension strategy instruction, for the most part Amy was doing very little coaching.

It took about three months before Amy and her colleagues figured out that they needed to pencil specific times for coaching teachers into the schedule. They decided to schedule Amy for classroom coaching on Thursday mornings and for debriefing and planning follow-up lessons during the afternoon release time. Some teachers had to give up the reading support that Amy had been providing on Thursday mornings, but they knew that, in the long run, their students would benefit. With the new schedule in place, Amy could provide consistent, ongoing coaching all year for every grade level. Here's how it worked: Amy would spend every Thursday either providing professional development or modeling lessons in classrooms, one grade level at a time. The school even held a Guided Reading Training Day, during which Amy conducted 90-minute blocks of preplanning, lesson modeling, and debriefing, using the four-step ITE coaching model.

Summary

It may seem contradictory after everything you've just read, but we are now going to quote Ralph Waldo Emerson: "A foolish consistency is the hobgoblin of little minds." In coaching, an example of foolish consistency would be to make a plan, carry it out with fidelity, evaluate the plan as you go, realize that it just isn't working—and continue doing the same thing. This whole chapter is about *wise* consistency—that is, consistency that supports and sustains participants in a coaching effort.

Keep It Strong
with Data

The wolf was so angry that he dashed with all his force
against the wall and tried to knock it down. But it was
too strong and well built.

—The Three Little Pigs

Like a house, a good coaching initiative must have supports in place to hold it together—only in this case, the supports are made up of data rather than concrete and steel. No matter how often the furniture (practices) or residents (teachers and students) change, the supports (data) help the structure stay strong.

The Blueprint

Consider the following all-too-familiar scenario. A district administrative team finds that School A has over 90 percent proficiency in reading. Because this school has been using Strategy X, the team decides that all the other district schools should drop what they're doing and implement the same strategy. However, the team neglects to examine the data closely to see if the strategy is having the same effect with all students across the board. Meanwhile, School B in the same district is trying out a different strategy, and its data show significant gains for a specific subgroup of students over three years—but because all of the students are nowhere near the 90 percent proficiency level of School A, School B is directed to drop its initiative under the false assumption that what works for one building works for all.

Just as contractors must work from a good blueprint to build a solid house, you as a coach must have a good blueprint for strong literacy coaching. To determine the purpose of your coaching, examine both standardized test scores and classroom assessment data. If the data indicate that students have particular trouble with vocabulary, for example, then one purpose of the coaching initiative should be to help students in that area.

The Materials

If you want to build a strong, upscale house, you need to pick the best materials available. In literacy coaching, these "materials" are the practices you use to reach your goals. Choosing those practices is one of the most important things you will do. Sometimes, you have the practices thrust upon you by administrators, in which case you simply do the best you can. If you are lucky enough to be able to help select the practices, our advice is to consult the research and experts but also to use your own common sense and knowledge about your students to inform your decision.

The Workers

Joe's late again, Mandy and Hal talk on their cell phones all day, and Pete doesn't seem to know a ball-peen hammer from a plumb bob. In a case like this, a crew boss has two options: firing the workers or using a combination of inspiration, perks, and authority to get them to do a good job. As a literacy coach, firing your workers (that is, the teachers) just isn't an option, so it's up to you to support them—to teach them, inspire them, appreciate them, and celebrate their accomplishments.

Best Practices

Imagine home builders approaching their task by randomly assembling a large pile of bricks, steel beams, and wood and then pouring concrete over everything. Clearly, procuring the best materials doesn't automatically guarantee the best results; it's also important to know what to *do* with those good materials. If those who are using them are well trained and knowledgeable, and if they monitor their work as they go to see if any modifications are needed, then excellent results will ensue.

We learn very quickly that what is taught isn't always what is learned or put into practice. For whatever reason, teachers may ignore what they've been taught or adapt it to fit their own ideas and situations. Keep in mind that adult learners are relevancy oriented: they need to know not only the goal but also why it's important. Don't ever expect them to "just do it." Literacy coaching requires you to implement with fidelity the best practices you have selected.

Monitoring and Flexibility

Even if you have the best blueprint, materials, and workers, it's still necessary to monitor the implementation of a plan and be ready to make adjustments when things don't go as planned. We know that building the strongest literacy coaching initiative takes more than relying on just standardized and classroom assessment data. Monitoring should be a continuous process of paying attention to various data sources and making adjustments. If you don't pay attention to what these sources actually tell you and respond to missteps, all your other efforts may be wasted or robbed of their full potential.

Maintenance

A house that is strong at the beginning won't stay that way forever. Regularly scheduled maintenance can ensure that small problems don't become huge problems.

Even though it sometimes seemed to be taking time from our coaching, we scheduled weekly maintenance meetings. They were well worth the time it took. We were able to identify small problems before they became huge problems.

In addition to our weekly maintenance meetings, we organized monthly meetings with the key teachers from each school, who were able to identify problems that we would perhaps never have known about. There were monthly meetings for all of the teachers, too, during which they would divide up by grade levels to share ideas, questions, and solutions. Sometimes these meetings slipped into gripe sessions, but the principals who attended them managed to restrain the negativity. Of course, we learned as much from the negative comments as we did from the positive ones—if you want your coaching initiative to work, you can't listen to only the good news.

There will always be problems that don't fall under the maintenance plan because they weren't anticipated. In the case of a house, a tree may fall through the roof; in the case of a coaching initiative, a new principal may come into a school midyear and start changing all of the rules. When something like that happens, it's triage time. You can't just pretend that the rain isn't pouring through the roof.

When we designed the Reading Excellence initiative, we were so involved with teaching teachers how to conduct small-group reading instruction that we forgot about the students who were expected to work independently. Left to their own devices, teachers were assigning those students a lot of busywork. When we found this out, the literacy coaches put together some quality independent literacy activities for the teachers to use with these students. We did everything we could to make the strategies simple and easy to use, because we knew the teachers had enough on their plates already.

Working with Data

There are two extremes to the data continuum. At one end are the gamblers, who make decisions based on the yearly "big test" and by gut feeling rather than on continuous, ongoing assessment. At the other end are the data fanatics, who collect data about every little thing in their zeal to meet standards. When analyzing data, it helps to visualize the applicable cautions as they would appear on a prescription information sheet:

Name of Ingredient: Informal reading test.

General Uses: To assess student reading progress and inform classroom reading instruction.

Directions: Follow the directions for using this assessment that your literacy coach provided. Before administering the test, activate prior knowledge and ask the student to predict what a passage will be about from the title alone. Next, tell the student that he or she will read the passage and then retell it, as well as answer questions about it. Watch the student carefully and take notes on reading behavior. Complete the assessment as directed by your literacy coach.

Caution: Other data results may interact with this information. INFORM YOUR TEACHERS OR ADMINISTRATOR of all other diagnostic data and anecdotal information that you are using. DO NOT USE THIS TEST IF YOU INTEND TO STANDARDIZE IT IN YOUR DISTRICT. If misused, data could lead to false conclusions about student learning.

Benefits: For teachers and parents, increased, detailed information about their students' reading; for students, increased abilities in inferential thinking and in determining importance during reading.

Possible Side Effects: This test has no known negative side effects unless overused. Symptoms of overdose may include teaching to the test and too much prompting during student retelling.

Ensuring That Data Fit Your Purpose

You must make sure that your data collection fits the original purpose of your coaching initiative and that you have a plan for using it. Be careful not to overload teachers with irrelevant paperwork, as this will create a disconnect among the data, instruction, and student learning, and teachers will rebel. For example, a teacher approached Amy once about the implementation log she was supposed to fill out. "It takes me longer to fill out this piece of paper than it does for me to teach the lesson," she said: "I really don't want to fill this thing out anymore." The teacher was right. The original purpose for the log—to get teachers implementing—had been breached. If teachers were teaching but not filling out the log, then we were getting a false picture of actual implementation.

Very often, data requested from a school by a district can also be used by the school itself. Here's an example. Amy was once hired to provide coaching for middle and high school teachers in teaching comprehension strategies. The teachers were also trained in peer coaching by their on-site curriculum director. The district wanted to monitor how well the schools were implementing the comprehension strategies and peer coaching, so Amy made a simple chart showing the number of teachers at each grade level participating in peer coaching. She then coded each log according to the level of comprehension-strategy instruction it exhibited. The data gleaned from the logs indicated that some teachers taught the comprehension strategies as Amy had directed, while others changed the lesson to such a degree that the intended strategy was not even being taught.

The next time Amy went to the district, she shared the data with teachers as well as administrators and restated the importance of teaching strategies as shown during professional development. Without the implementation data, both the teachers and the district administrators would have had a false picture of implementation at the schools. Implementation logs that are reflective in nature, such as the one shown in Figure 5.1, offer particularly useful data.

Additional Data Sources

Other important data sources include expert friends and administrators, external professional development providers, and university professors. When we were implementing the Reading Excellence initiative, our expert friend, Penny Beed, a professor at the University of Northern Iowa, served as an advisor and provided us with needed expertise. Principals can visit classrooms to monitor implementation of new practices and suggest how to follow up. External professional development providers can let you know how initiatives at your school compare to others around the country or world.

FIGURE 5.1	Sample Implementation Log

School _____ Teacher _____ Grade ____ Date ____
Group (circle one): GR - TGR - Shared Reading - PK - K
Book Title/Level _____

1. Check the part of the lesson sequence you are describing:
____ Setting the Scene ____ Picture Walk ____ Oral/Silent Read
____ Return to the Text ____ Response

What did you do in this part of the lesson? _____

What did you say in this part of the lesson? _____

What did the students do? _____

What did the students say? _____

2. My actions had the following instructional implications:

_____

3. My decision to take these actions was guided by
____ Professional book   ____ Workshop or conference
____ Curricular requirements   ____ Demonstration lesson (live/video)
____ Other
Because: _____

4. My next step will be to do the following:

_____

5. In the last five school days, have you worked with peer coaching partner(s) to plan your small-group reading instruction?

____ Yes ____ No   If "Yes," how many times? _____

6. In the last five school days, have you demonstrated the teaching of a reading group (live or on tape) for peer coaching partner(s)?

____ Yes ____ No   If "Yes," how many times? _____

Keeping Data in Perspective

In her book *How to Use Action Research in the Self-Renewing School* (1994), Emily Calhoun offers a Schoolwide Action Research matrix that has been adapted by the Iowa Department of Education to help make sure data are used the right way. We used this matrix and came up with the following five target questions to keep our data use relevant and focused:

1. Where is the information?
2. What kind of information is it?
3. What is the information telling us?
4. What will we do with the information?
5. Do we really need this information?

Asking these questions will help focus your data use.

Managing the Data

Managing data can be all-consuming, so make sure that responsibility is shared. If you have a leadership team, the teachers involved can help. It is helpful to explicitly state who will do what tasks. If you are working with several schools, have a portable file sectioned by grade level. Decide what data are useful and enter them in a spreadsheet. Formal assessments such as standardized test scores often come already organized for us by the testing company or district, but are they easy to understand? Can teachers look at them and know what the scores are telling them? If not, reorganize the data.

As the literacy coach, you can save your teachers and leadership teams time by organizing data ahead of time for them. You may even want to create an easy-to-read visual that teachers can understand quickly. A goal at one of Amy's schools was to increase the amount of time spent each day on small-group reading instruction. To track progress, teachers recorded the number of minutes they spent on small-group reading instruction in an implementation log. They then turned their logs in to Amy, who organized the data into a simple graph comparing the log data with research on optimal small-group reading instruction time from the Center for the Improvement of Early Reading Achievement (CIERA) (see Figure 5.2).

Summary

Too often, we invest a great amount of time and effort in planning our initiative but neglect to build in ways to sustain it over time. The considerations outlined in this chapter will ensure that your literacy coaching initiative is strong, sturdy, and able to stand the test of time—just like a well-built house. Remember to

- Define your purpose and stick to it
- Select materials that match your purpose and people who can help achieve it
- Be deliberate in your work and remain flexible
- Analyze data to monitor progress, but don't collect irrelevant information

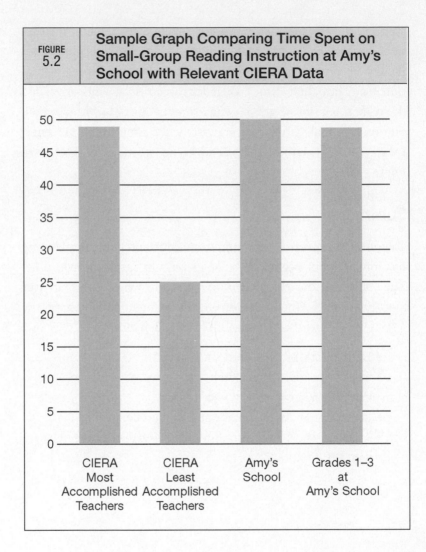

FIGURE 5.2

Sample Graph Comparing Time Spent on Small-Group Reading Instruction at Amy's School with Relevant CIERA Data

6

Seek First to Understand

Grant that I may not so much seek . . . to be understood as to understand.

—*St. Francis of Assisi*

The Seven Habits of Highly Effective People (1989) by Stephen R. Covey is one of the few books that has changed our everyday thinking forever. Our favorite habit is the fifth: "Seek first to understand, then to be understood" (p. 237). Before reading Covey's book, we had always assumed that it was our job as professional developers to provide people with information and understanding and then get them to act on it by doing things our way. Covey's book gave us a whole new perspective, reminding us to fight against that voice inside that says, "You know what's best, you have the education, and you've done the research. Now you just have to make your teachers do what's right." That, of course, would be "what's right" according to us, not the teachers. Instead, your job is to help teachers do *their* best. When we have sought first to understand before being understood, we have learned some interesting and valuable lessons.

Most teachers feel highly responsible for their students' learning and believe they are teaching them well. A tricky thing about really effective coaching is helping these teachers hold their old beliefs up to examination and, if necessary, adopt a new way of thinking. For example, it is currently widely accepted among reading experts that the "round robin" reading strategy not only is useless but may actually do harm (Opitz & Rasinski, 1998). Yet many of the teachers we've met grew up with the strategy and may think of it as the only way to "get through the text." Seeking to understand is key to effective coaching, so it helps to listen to the teacher before any work begins. Once the coach finds out why the teacher believes that round robin reading is effective, the coach can model other, more productive ways of "getting through the text" with the students. The teacher can step back, watch the students, and judge the effectiveness of the coach's strategy versus the effectiveness of round robin reading. Quite often, the students' positive reaction to the new way is what convinces the teacher to change strategies. In such cases, teachers need new ideas and the coach's support implementing them.

Teachers have seen a lot of programs come down the pike, stay for a brief time, and disappear. They might think that if they just hold out for a year or even a month, what you're promoting will go away too. Often they have every reason to believe this, because it has happened many times before. You have two responsibilities in this situation. First, you need to convince the teachers that what you have to offer is based on solid research. (It doesn't hurt to let them know that it's supported by their administrators, too.) Second, you need to convince them that the strategy you are imparting is not going to go away.

By coaching teachers to reflect when trying out new ways of teaching, you can put the power to excel in their hands. When you listen to what they tell you, you can seek out research data and other information to help them make decisions. This can only be accomplished by being consistent and good at what you do. Teachers may still have doubts about the longevity of certain strategies, but they may also begin to see that they can benefit from what you have to offer. By the time a strategy becomes entrenched, teachers will have forgotten that they ever thought it was just another passing educational fancy. (They may also have forgotten that it wasn't their idea all along!)

Just as you respect others in your life who don't share your opinions, you must also respect the teachers with whom you work. It helps for you to put yourself in their shoes. When you think about what your reaction would be in a given situation, you begin to understand what teachers want: to examine what you teach them and accept, reject, or (in most cases) adapt it to what they already know. A wise coach respects this process and the time it takes. The wisest coach even admits that sometimes the teachers are right and he or she needs to be the one to make a change.

How many times has this happened to you: You're doing your best to express your views to someone, trying really hard to communicate, when suddenly you realize that the other person is not really listening, just waiting to talk. When it's the other person's turn to speak, you get no sense that he or she is responding to what you have said. It's the same feeling you get when you hear politicians "answer" questions with already-prepared statements.

Never mistake being quiet while someone else is talking for true listening. When you really listen, you actually *hear* what the other person is saying and integrate what you hear into your own thinking. That's what it takes even to begin to understand another person's point of view. If you *really listen* to teachers, you may hear pleas for you to change your approach to coaching. For example, you may come to understand that you're moving too fast or pushing too hard. A teacher's anger or resistance may simply be born of frustration.

One of the benefits of careful listening is that it lets you know when teachers are misunderstanding something. We've noticed that there can be several misunderstandings or "re-understandings" between the time teachers receive information and coaching and the time they implement new procedures. As an example, the major innovation in the Reading Excellence initiative was the implementation of small-group reading instruction. Yet even after teachers had received a full year of training, it was still possible to walk into some classrooms and find "small" reading groups of up to 15 students!

Imagine the following scenario. You have been suffering from a backache for several weeks, so you make an appointment with your doctor. When she comes into the examining room, she says good morning and hands you a prescription. You are amazed to see that the prescription is preprinted rather than written out in the customary scrawl. As the doctor starts to leave the room, you try to stop her. "Don't you want to know what's wrong with me?" you ask. Barely pausing on her way out of the door, the doctor responds, "Oh, that won't be necessary. This is what I'm prescribing for all my patients. It's the latest thing. I'm sure it will make you feel better."

Like the doctor above, coaches too often prescribe solutions without first diagnosing the problems. Of course, it's not as if we can give the teachers a pre-test to find out what they need to learn. In most cases we have only our own observations to guide us, and we are often tempted to ignore even those. *We're on a mission to improve instruction for the students, so get out of our way; we're coming through!*

As you work with teachers, take notes on what they say and do. Then, use these observation data to individually or collectively plan coaching or other professional development. When you collect and use both observational data and hard data, the result will be tailored prescriptions for effectiveness, rather than one-size-fits-all solutions.

Summary

We encourage you to treat your teachers with understanding and respect—to listen to them, learn from them, and make use of what you learn. You must be aware, you must be reflective, and above all, you must seek first to understand.

Conclusion

This book is about using the fundamentals of literacy coaching to build a strong initiative that *works* for everyone involved. It's also about simplifying what can often seem like a very complex matter.

Be prepared. Make friends. Teach. Be consistent. Keep it strong. Seek first to understand. Running through these fundamentals are the following common threads—the warp and the woof, for those weavers among you—that strengthen the fabric of literacy coaching.

Excellence. Start with the expectation that you are going to have an excellent program, and choose excellence in every decision along the way. Our teachers and students deserve it.

Planning ahead. Be ready for what's coming, or know that the unexpected is going to come. Being proactive will save a lot of time and a lot of grief; in the end, it may even save your program.

Simplicity. Initiatives that are unnecessarily complex and difficult do not fare well, because teachers get overwhelmed and exhausted, and nothing happens. The purpose and vision are buried in the details. Though all of the fundamentals may have been considered, such initiatives are done in by their own elaborateness.

Flexibility. Your program needs to stretch and adapt to meet changing needs.

Monitoring. Put your observations to use and make changes to improve.

Data. Decisions about procedures, professional development, and coaching individual teachers must be based on formal and informal data.

Perseverance. Push on through unforeseen difficulties—through changes to staff, administration, and even best practices.

People. Without considering the *humanity* of those involved in the initiative, your fabric will fade, shrink, and fray.

Celebration. It is crucial to celebrate milestones. Take time to appreciate the teachers. Have a little party just for yourself! Too often, we pay attention only to immediate problems or the work of the day. Don't wait for standardized test results or for the school year to end. Congratulate yourselves on progress, no matter how incremental.

We celebrate this opportunity to share with you our experiences with making literacy coaching work. We hope you find it a practical reference as you begin your journey, too. For those of you who are just starting out, be reassured that you can make it work. Celebrate having the chance of your professional lifetime! For those of you who have already started the journey, celebrate your existing effort! For all coaches, celebrate the fact that you are facilitating meaningful, worthwhile support for teachers! We celebrate the fact that you are committed to literacy coaching and have the opportunity to see what excellent, quality professional development can do for your school or district. Frankly, we're a little jealous.

Bibliography

Allington, R. L. (2002). What I've learned about effective reading instruction from a decade of studying exemplary classroom teachers. *Phi Delta Kappan, 83*(10), 740–747.

Barsade, S. G. (2002). The ripple effect: Emotional contagion and its influence on group behavior. *Administrative Science Quarterly, 47*(4), 644–675.

Beed, P. L., Hawkins, E. M., & Roller, C. M. (1991). Moving learners toward independence: The power of scaffolded instruction. *The Reading Teacher, 44*(9), 648–655.

Bruner, J. S. (1975). The ontogenesis of speech acts. *Journal of Child Language, 2,* 1–40.

Calhoun, E. (1994). *How to use action research in the self-renewing school.* Alexandria, VA: Association for Supervision and Curriculum Development.

Carran, N. (2000). *Critical attributes of staff development for student achievement.* Des Moines: Iowa Department of Education.

Center for the Improvement of Early Reading Achievement. (2000). *Beating the odds in teaching all students to read: Lessons from effective schools and accomplished teachers.* Ann Arbor: University of Michigan. (ERIC Document Reproduction Service No. ED 450 352)

Costa, A., & Garmston, R. (1994). *Cognitive coaching: A foundation for Renaissance schools.* Norwood, MA: Christopher-Gordon.

Covey, S. (1989). *The 7 habits of highly effective people.* New York: Simon & Schuster.

Cunningham, P., Hall, D., & Sigmon, C. (2000). *The teacher's guide to the Four Blocks.* Greensboro, NC: Carson-Dellosa.

Dodd, A., & Rosenbaum, E. (1986, January). Learning communities for curriculum and staff development. *Phi Delta Kappan, 67*(5), 380–384.

Dole, J. (2004). The changing role of the reading specialist in school reform. *The Reading Teacher, 57*(5), 461–471.

Eisner, E. W., & Vallance, E. (Eds.). (1974). *Conflicting conceptions of curriculum.* Berkeley, CA: McCutchan.

Erickson, L. G. (1995). *Supervision of literacy programs: Teachers as grass-roots change agents.* Needham Heights, MA: Allyn & Bacon.

Fenstermacher, G. (1993). The elicitation and reconstruction of practical arguments in teaching. *Journal of Curriculum Studies, 25*(2), 101–104.

Fountas, I. C., & Pinnell, G. S. (1996). *Guided reading: Good first teaching for all.* Portsmouth, NH: Heinemann.

Fullan, M. (1985). Change processes and strategies at the local school level. *Elementary School Journal, 85,* 391–421.

Fullan, M., & Hargreaves, A. (1991). *What's worth fighting for in your school.* New York: Teachers College Press.

Goleman, D. (1995). *Emotional intelligence: Why it can matter more than IQ for character, health and lifelong achievement.* New York: Bantam Books.

Goleman, D. (2006, September). The socially intelligent leader. *Educational Leadership, 64*(1), 76–81.

Hall, G. E., & Hord, S. M. (2006). *Implementing change: Patterns, principles, and potholes.* Boston: Pearson Education.

Harvey, S., & Goodvis, A. (2000). *Strategies that work: Teaching comprehension to enhance understanding.* Portland, ME: Stenhouse Publishers.

Hunter, M. C. (1986). *Mastery teaching.* El Segundo, CA: TIP Publications.

International Reading Association. (2004). *The role and qualifications of the reading coach in the United States.* Available: http://www.reading.org/downloads/positions/ps1065_reading_coach.pdf

Iowa Department of Education. (2005). *The Iowa professional development model training manual.* Available: http://www.iowa.gov/educate/pdmtm/state.html

Joyce, B., & Showers, B. (1988). *Student achievement through staff development.* New York: Longman.

Joyce, B., & Showers, B. (1995). *Student achievement through staff development: Fundamentals of school renewal* (2nd ed.). New York: Longman.

Knowles, M. (1990). *The adult learner: A neglected species* (4th ed.). Houston, TX: Gulf Publishing Company.

Lieberman, A., & Miller, L. (1984). *Teachers, their world, and their work: Implications for school improvement.* Alexandria, VA: Association for Supervision and Curriculum Development.

Opitz, M. F., & Rasinski, T. V. (1998). *Goodbye round robin: 25 effective oral reading strategies.* Portsmouth, NH: Heinemann.

Patti, J., & Tobin, J. (2003). *Smart school leaders: Leading with emotional intelligence.* Dubuque, IA: Kendall-Hunt.

Pearson, P. D., & Gallagher, M. C. (1983). The instruction of reading comprehension. *Contemporary Educational Psychology, 8,* 317–344.

Raphael, T. E. (1984, January). Teaching learners about sources of information for answering comprehension questions. *Journal of Reading, 27,* 303–311.

Richardson, V. (2003, January). The dilemmas of professional development. *Phi Delta Kappan, 84*(5), 403.

Saunders-Smith, G. (2003). *The ultimate guided reading how-to book.* Tucson, AZ: Zephyr Press.

Schmoker, M. (1996). *Results: The key to continuous school improvement*. Alexandria, VA: Assocation for Supervision and Curriculum Development.

Schmoker, M. (2002, Spring). Up and away. *Journal of Staff Development, 23*(2), 10–13.

Showers, B., & Joyce, B. (1996). The evolution of peer coaching. *Educational Leadership, 53*(6), 12–16.

Tidwell, D. L., Hoewing, B. L., & Ko-Bras, H. (2003). *Remedial reading and tutoring* (6th ed.). Upper Saddle River, NJ: Pearson.

Van Pelt, J., & Poparad, M. A. (2006, April). Revamping reading: One district moves from a patchwork to a coordinated curriculum and coaching to improve reading skills among elementary students systemwide. *The School Administrator, 63*(4), 31–34.

Vygotsky, L. S. (1978). *Mind in society: The development of higher psychological processes*. Cambridge, MA: Harvard University Press.

Index

....

....

About the Authors

 **Amy Sandvold** has been a Title I reading teacher and served as a full-time literacy coach at rural, urban, and suburban elementary schools. She has also served as a consultant for the Iowa Department of Education, taught several courses at the University of Northern Iowa, and presented on numerous literacy and school improvement topics at regional and international reading conferences.

Amy holds an MA in education and is working toward her Advanced Studies Certificate in education leadership at the University of Northern Iowa. She has written for *The Thinking Classroom*, a publication of the International Reading Association, and she currently teaches 3rd grade at Cedar Heights Elementary School in Cedar Falls, Iowa. She lives in Cedar Falls with her husband, Jeff, and children, Houston, Andrew, Lauren, and Anna. She can be reached at Sandvold@cfu.net.

 **Maelou Baxter** has worked as a Title I reading teacher and consultant, a Reading Excellence grant project coordinator, and an instructor at the University of Northern Iowa, Wartburg College, and Upper Iowa University. She holds a BA in English, an MA in education, and an EdD, and has presented on various literacy topics at reading conferences. Though currently retired, Maelou continues to follow her literacy interests and her avocation as a "professional learner." She volunteers for the Friends of the Library and travels with her husband, Ken, with whom she lives in Cedar Falls, Iowa. She has three grown children, Jennifer, Karen, and Jeff, and five grandchildren, Jessica, Lincoln, Abbie, Zach, and Zoë. She may be reached at mbax@cfu.net.

Related ASCD Resources: Literacy Coaching

At the time of publication, the following ASCD resources were available; for the most up-to-date information about ASCD resources, go to www.ascd.org. ASCD stock numbers are noted in parentheses.

Books

Creating Dynamic Schools through Mentoring, Coaching, and Collaboration by Judy F. Carr, Nancy Herman, and Douglas E. Harris (#103021)

How to Plan and Implement a Peer Coaching Program by Pam Robbins (#6119114)

Student Achievement through Staff Development by Bruce R. Joyce and Beverly Showers (#102003)

Transforming Schools: Creating a Culture of Continuous Improvement by Allison Zmuda, Robert Kuklis, and Everett Kline (#103112)

Mixed Media

Creating the Capacity for Change by Jody Mason Westbrook and Valerie Spiser-Albert (ASCD action tool; #702118)

Making Mentoring Work by Laura Lipton and Bruce Wellman (ASCD action tool; #703108)

Using Data to Assess Your Reading Program by Emily Calhoun (one book and one CD-ROM; #102268)

For additional resources, visit us on the World Wide Web (http://www.ascd.org), send an e-mail message to member@ascd.org, call the ASCD Service Center (1-800-933-ASCD or 703-578-9600, then press 2), send a fax to 703-575-5400, or write to Information Services, ASCD, 1703 N. Beauregard St., Alexandria, VA 22311-1714 USA.